To Pen, Noo and Kieran

THE ESSENCE OF

STRUCTURED SYSTEMS ANALYSIS TECHNIQUES

THE ESSENCE OF COMPUTING SERIES

Published Titles

The Essence of Programming using C++
The Essence of Program Design
The Essence of Artificial Intelligence
The Essence of Discrete Mathematics
The Essence of Human Computer Interaction
The Essence of Logic
The Essence of Databases
The Essence of Structured Systems Analysis Techniques

Forthcoming Titles

The Essence of Z
The Essence of Compilers

THE ESSENCE OF

STRUCTURED SYSTEMS ANALYSIS TECHNIQUES

Gary Griffiths

Prentice Hall Europe

LONDON   NEW YORK   TORONTO   SYDNEY   TOKYO
SINGAPORE   MADRID   MEXICO CITY   MUNICH   PARIS

First published 1998 by
Prentice Hall Europe
Campus 400, Maylands Avenue
Hemel Hempstead
Hertfordshire, HP2 7EZ
A division of
Simon & Schuster International Group

Typeset in 10/12 pt Times
by Photoprint, Torquay

Printed and bound in Great Britain by
MPG Books Ltd, Bodmin, Cornwall

Library of Congress Cataloging-in-Publication Data

Available from the publisher

British Library Cataloguing in Publication Data

A catalogue record for this book is available from
the British Library

ISBN 0–13–749847–0

---

1 2 3 4 5   02 01 00 99 98

Contents

Foreword

As the consulting editor for the Essence of Computing Series it is my role to encourage the production of well-focused, high-quality textbooks at prices which students can afford. Since most computing courses are modular in structure, we aim to produce books which will cover the essential material for a typical module.

I want to maintain a consistent style for the series so that whenever you pick up an Essence book you know what to expect. For example, each book contains important features such as end-of-chapter summaries and exercises and a glossary of terms, if appropriate. Of course, the quality of the series depends crucially on the skills of its authors and all the books are written by lecturers who have honed their material in the classroom. Each book in the series takes a pragmatic approach and emphasises practical examples and case studies.

Our aim is that each book will become essential reading material for students attending core modules in computing. However, we expect students to want to go beyond the Essence books and so all books contain guidance on further reading and related work.

Systems Analysis is a key component of the software development process and this book covers the major structured analysis techniques very thoroughly. The Introduction very clearly sets the scene and identifies the focus of this book. It is about developing information systems and the core of the book concentrates on data flow diagrams, data modelling, data dictionaries and entity life histories. The material is clearly presented, illustrated with substantial examples and well thought-out exercises are provided to test the reader's understanding of the techniques. I recommend this book as an excellent text for a module on systems analysis and I look forward to using it myself!

RAY WELLAND
Department of Computing Science
University of Glasgow
(e-mail: ray@dcs.gla.ac.uk)

CHAPTER 1

Introduction

The main aim of this book is to help people develop practical skills in the techniques of structured systems analysis. In this chapter, the scope of the book is defined and the history of structured methods is charted. We'll look at the types of method that we will be studying, and those that we will not; the stages of developing a computer system that we will be concentrating on, and those that we will not; and the types of application that we will be considering, and those that we will not. We'll also discuss why structured methods were developed in the first place, the techniques that are associated with them and how they might be supported with software tools.

1.1 In the beginning . . .

If we consider how computer systems were developed before structured methods, we can see a clear need for improvement. If we're honest about it, there really were no methods before structured methods. There were only vague ideas about a development life cycle, where each system went through a series of stages. At each stage, various tasks were carried out that resulted in certain deliverables. But the tasks were not well defined and the deliverables were often enormous written reports that were virtually incomprehensible to everybody but the author. The tasks and deliverables in the life cycle varied widely from company to company and there was no standardization across the industry.

Life cycles also varied from company to company, but there was more of a consensus here and a typical life cycle was like the one shown in Figure 1.1. First, a feasibility study was carried out by a systems analyst. This looked at the technical feasibility and economic viability of the proposed system. A quick investigation of the requirements was done, together with a technical assessment and a cost–benefit analysis. This was then written up in a report that went to management for a decision.

If this was favourable, a full investigation of the system was carried out in the systems analysis phase. This was done mostly by the analyst talking to the people concerned, but sometimes there were helpful supporting documents to read and occasionally the analyst even did some of the jobs for a short while.

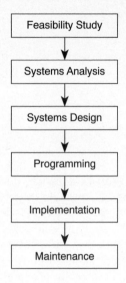

Figure 1.1

Another report was prepared which specified what was needed, but not how this would be achieved.

This was addressed in the next phase, systems design. Here the work became more technical and the main tasks were to develop program specifications, file layouts, etc. In the programming phase the programs were written and tested. In the implementation phase, data was loaded into files and users changed over from the old to the new system.

Finally, maintenance was carried out on the operational system. This covered both bug-fixing and enhancement and was an enormous drain on the computer department's resources. Typically two thirds of their time was spent on this activity rather than on new development, which created an applications backlog of several years.

In the early phases of this life cycle, there were really no tools or techniques to help at all. The analyst was often swamped by the sheer volume of information, with no way to structure or order it, apart from common sense. Also, the users of the system couldn't help much, because at that time, in the mid-1970s, very few had any idea of what computer systems could actually offer them. Communication between the analyst and the user was either by conversation or by voluminous written reports and it is no surprise that things were often missed or misunderstood.

To make matters worse, technology was advancing quickly at this point in time and there was great pressure to provide systems that were ever more complex. Previously, batch processing using conventional files had been the norm, but the use of database and transaction processing was spreading fast.

Table 1.1

Stage	Relative cost
Analysis	1
Design	2
Programming	5
Implementation	20
Operation	50

Boehm (1976) published some research that emphasized the need for improved techniques in the early part of the life cycle. It concerned the relative costs of correcting errors at various stages. In Table 1.1 we can see that it costs twice as much to correct an error once the system has got to the design stage as it would have done if it was spotted at the analysis stage. This gets dramatically worse, and it costs five times as much in programming. . . twenty times as much at implementation. . . and fifty times as much once the system has gone live.

So, for all these reasons, the hunt was on for better tools and techniques, particularly in the early phases of the life cycle. In the early days of developing computer systems, the only tools used were compilers, to develop the program code, and there were no techniques. In fact, the first stage of the life cycle was often programming, which contributed in no small measure to what many were calling the 'software crisis' described above. In fact, programming was seen as a creative (if not artistic) pursuit by many of its early practitioners, who often described their obscure and unmaintainable program code as 'elegant'.

However, it was obvious to many people that this had to change and in the late 1960s the term 'software engineering' was first coined. The basic shift of philosophy here was to see the production of software as an engineering process rather than a creative one. This fuelled the desire to develop a life cycle to guide the development process, together with techniques to populate the life cycle, and tools to support the techniques. The previous attempts at producing computer systems merely by churning out program code were derided as 'hacking'.

The first basic life cycle that evolved was similar to that in Figure 1.1. This was often referred to as the 'waterfall model' because the development flowed from stage to stage. This has been much criticized since for its lack of iteration etc., and these criticisms are valid. There has been much research in this area since and many alternatives have been proposed, but the waterfall model still provides us with the simplest, clearest overview of the set of activities that must be carried out to develop a computer system.

The first part of the life cycle to be better understood was the programming phase. It was proposed by Dijkstra and others (see Dahl *et al.*, 1972) that the control structures in virtually all programming languages could be categorized as sequence, selection or iteration. The importance of this insight into the nature of computer programs has proved to be huge and it is still very important today. It gave rise to the first 'structured' technique to be used in developing computer systems, perhaps the first technique of any type: structured programming. The word 'structured' was used to try to convey a methodical, ordered approach which proceeded 'top-down'. These ideas were also applied to data successfully by Jackson (1975), and several structured programming techniques were promoted, including the first graphical techniques.

For example, Figure 1.2 is a small example of a Jackson structure diagram as used in Jackson Structured Programming (JSP). Here, the stock adjustments program is broken down into a sequence of modules: initialization, followed by the main body, followed by finalization. The main body is an iteration of processing stock adjustments (the asterisk denotes an iteration). This is then broken down into a selection: for each stock adjustment, stock is either incremented or decremented (the circle denotes selection). JSP will not be pursued further in this book as we are dealing with systems analysis.

These approaches proved very popular and, for reasons mentioned earlier, attempts were made to apply them earlier in the life cycle. The next step was to address the life cycle stage before programming: systems design. Yourdon and Constantine (1975) proposed structure charts in the mid-1970s. These were

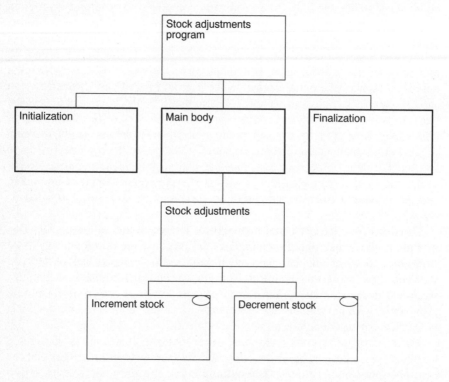

Figure 1.2

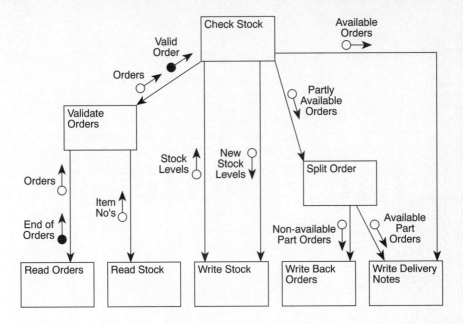

Figure 1.3

an attempt to graphically depict the sub-components of a program (procedures, functions, etc.) and the data and control that passed between them. For example, Figure 1.3 shows a structure chart for a 'Check Stock' process. We will not go into the notation in any detail here, except to say that the modules within the system are shown as oblong boxes and the connections between them as arrowed lines. Each of the connections has data and/or control associated with it in one or both directions. These are called couples. Data couples are shown as arrows with open circles and denote the passing of data between modules. Control couples are shown as arrows with filled circles and denote the passing of 'flags' between modules. We will look at structure charts in detail in Chapter 9.

The structured approach was then applied to the next phase back upstream, systems analysis, and data flow diagrams (or DFDs) were proposed in the late 1970s by various people associated with the Yourdon organization, principally De Marco (1978) and Gane and Sarson (1977). DFDs revolutionized systems analysis (although not overnight) and became the most popular software engineering technique.

Figure 1.4 shows an example of a DFD. Once you know that the squares are external entities, the circles are processes, the parallel lines are data stores and the arrows are data flows, these diagrams are almost self-explanatory. They have proved to be intuitive for non-technical people and provide an excellent way of communicating with a user. Also, the model is invaluable to the analyst

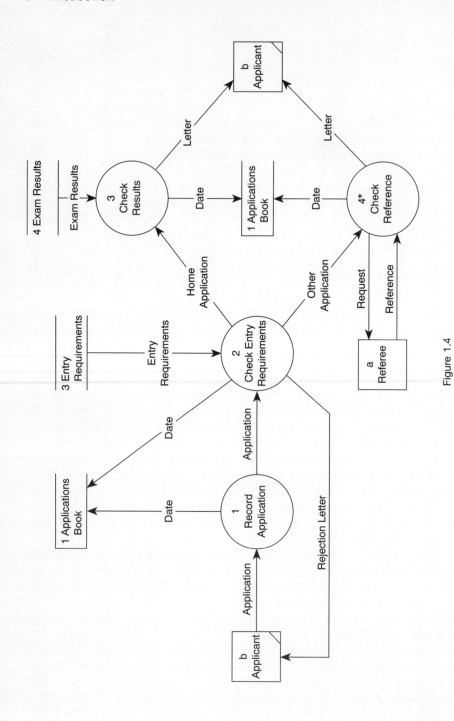

Figure 1.4

as a way of ordering the mass of information generated by the investigation. To facilitate this, the DFD is exploded. That is, each process on the DFD is examined to see if it would be useful to split it into sub-processes. If it would, a lower-level DFD is developed to model just that process. The processes of the child diagram could then be exploded in the same way if this was necessary.

From the DFD in Figure 1.4, we might decide to explode the process 'Check Reference'. This could give us a child diagram as shown in Figure 1.5. It is common to show the child diagram within the parent process. The objects connected at the upper level are arranged around the edge and are joined to individual objects on the lower-level diagram. This clearly shows the boundary between the levels. We will look at DFDs in detail in Chapters 2–4.

By this point in time there was an accepted life cycle, with several techniques at different stages, i.e. DFDs in systems analysis, structure charts in systems design and structured programming in the programming phase. Around now the first methods were proposed (often called 'methodologies', or to cynics 'mythologies'). These set down a life cycle and a set of integrated techniques to be used at different stages of the life cycle.

One of the first of the new structured systems analysis methods, and certainly the most enduring and popular, was the Yourdon method (De Marco, 1978). This covered the stages of systems analysis and systems design and used the techniques of data flow diagrams, a data dictionary and structure charts. We have already seen examples of the first and last of these, but not a data dictionary. This records details about items on the DFD, not only about data but also about processes. For example, we might have a data flow, Weekly Sales Report, on a DFD, as in Figure 1.6. In the data dictionary, we could develop a data structure for this report as follows:

```
WEEKLY-SALES REPORT
   AREA-SALES * (4)
      BRANCH-SALES * (3)
         BRANCH
         PROJECTED
         ACTUAL
         DIFFERENCE
      AREA-TOTALS
   COMPANY TOTALS
```

We won't go into the notation in detail here, but this could be read as follows. 'The Weekly Sales Report is made up of some area sales details, followed by company totals. For each area sales there's some branch sales details followed by an area total. For each branch sales, there's a branch, followed by a projected sales figure, followed by an actual sales figure, followed by a difference.' Each item in the structure would then be described further in terms

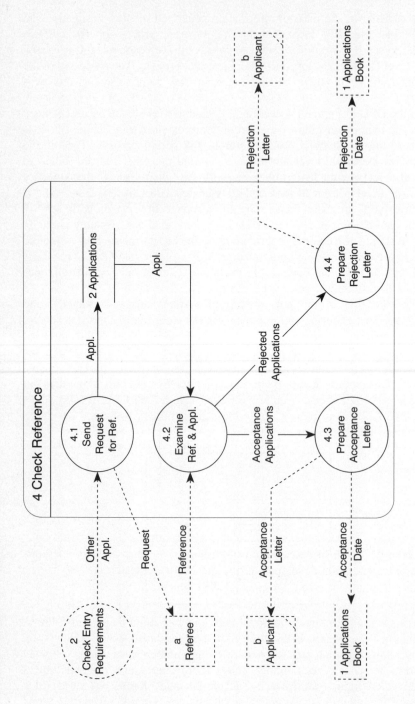

Figure 1.5

Figure 1.6

of, for example, length, values, ranges, and so on. We'll look at data descriptions in detail in Chapter 5.

We also record data about processes in the data dictionary. For example, the following is an outline specification that could be recorded in the data dictionary for a process 'Produce Weekly Sales Report'.

```
Produce Weekly Sales Report
    Write Headings
    DOWHILE more Weekly-Sales
        IF different Area-No
            Write Area-Totals
        ENDIF
        DO Output-Branch-Sales
    ENDDO
    Write Area-Totals
    Write Company-Totals
```

We'll look at process specification in detail in Chapter 6.

Gane and Sarson (1977) promoted a very similar method to Yourdon's, using similar techniques, at about the same time. Other methods dating from this period included Ross's (1977) structured analysis and design technique (SADT) and Jackson's (1983) Jackson Structured Design (JSD), which acted as a front end to his earlier Jackson Structured Programming (JSP). This might be considered to be the first generation of structured systems analysis methods.

The next generation developed during the 1980s. Research into information systems development (see Olle *et al.*, 1988) concluded that three views of a system were needed to model it effectively. These were process, data and time (or behaviour). While the Yourdon method contained elements of process and data, there was little argument that it was essentially process-orientated.

Entity relationship diagrams (ERDs) became popular at this time to model the data perspective. There are, broadly, two different styles of ERD notation. One of these is shown in Figure 1.7 where we have entities shown as oblong boxes and the relationships between them shown as diamonds. These diagrams

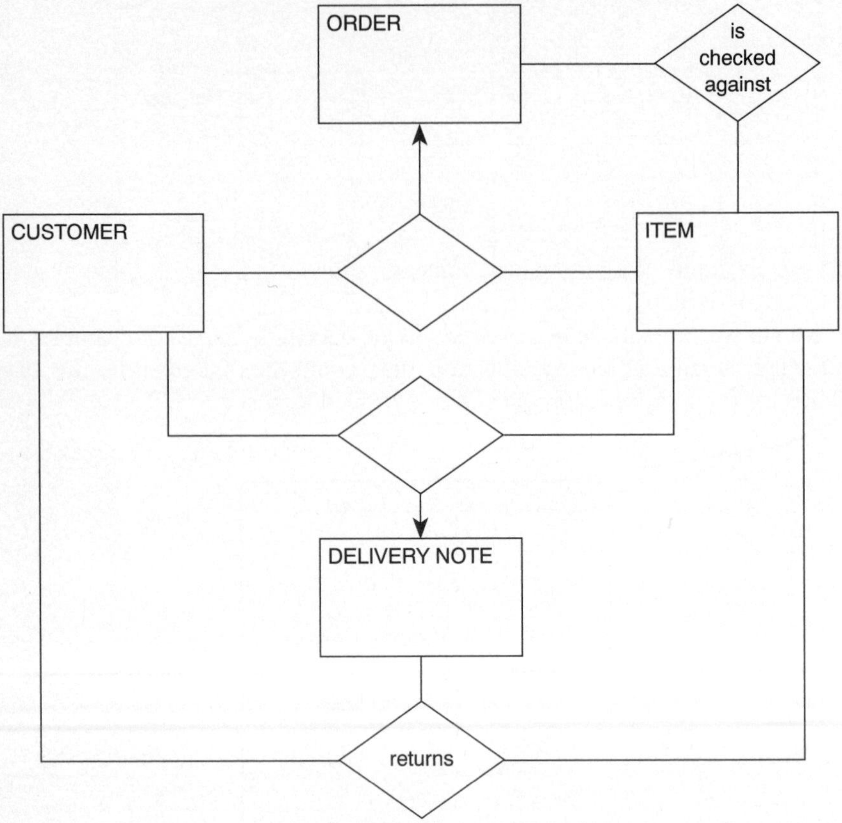

Figure 1.7

tend to be less intuitive, so we won't pursue them any further here, but we will be looking at ERDs in detail in Chapter 7.

One of the first methods to try to address all three perspectives more equally was structured systems analysis and design method (SSADM) (Ashworth and Slater, 1993; Robinson and Prior, 1995). This was developed in the UK for the government's Central Computing and Telecommunications Agency (CCTA) by Learmonth and Burchett Management Systems (LBMS). It used DFDs for the process perspective, ERDs for the data perspective and entity life histories (ELHs) for the behavioural perspective. The last of these was a new technique in that it modelled the behaviour of entities, but it leant heavily on JSP in terms of notation. Figure 1.8 gives an example of an ELH for a stock entity. We'll look at ELHs in detail in Chapter 8.

There followed a good deal of methods convergence in structured systems analysis, and at the end of the 1980s Yourdon brought out a new version of his method that was much more equal in its balance of perspectives (Yourdon,

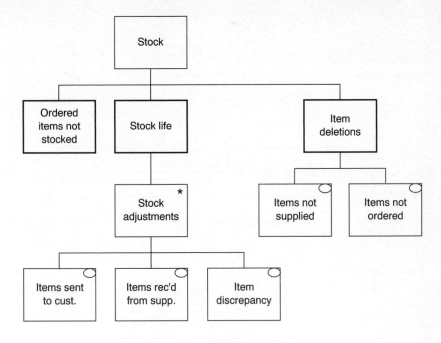

Figure 1.8

1989). Like SSADM, it used DFDs for the process perspective and ERDs for the data perspective. However, it employed a different technique, state transition diagrams (STDs), for the behavioural perspective.

Figure 1.9 gives an example of a STD. We won't go into the notation here, but we will be covering STDs in Chapter 8.

In addition to the difference in techniques there was also a distinction in the amount of freedom that they allowed. SSADM was very prescriptive about the steps and stages that a development must go through, whereas Yourdon was much more flexible.

Also, Yourdon was interested now not only in information systems, but in real-time systems as well (Ward and Mellor, 1986). By an information system we mean a computer system that processes data, stores it in files, and prints and displays information. Examples of information systems might be accounting, ordering, banking, purchasing, insurance, stock control, and so on. Real-time systems are strictly where the systems have to respond in real-time, i.e. immediately. Some information systems might be thought of as real-time systems, e.g. bank automatic teller machines (ATMs). However, in this book, we will use the term real-time to denote industrial control systems, where sensors and actuators might be used in industrial plant to sense temperature, open and close valves, and so on. In the updated Yourdon method, DFDs were extended to cater for real-time systems and state transition diagrams were

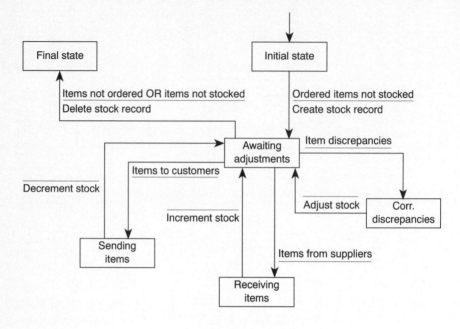

Figure 1.9

introduced to model their behaviour. The focus in SSADM has stayed with information systems.

In this book we are interested only in information systems and not in real-time systems. Real-time systems need a book of their own.

1.2 Structured walkthroughs

Techniques are of primary importance in this book, and methods are secondary. One technique used throughout the development stages that we haven't mentioned yet is the structured walkthrough (Yourdon, 1975). This is a meeting to review a product like a data flow diagram or a structure chart. At the walkthrough, the developer presents the product while the audience tries to identify any errors or omissions. The audience will usually consist of about four to six people. These are mostly development staff, but sometimes users will take part too, depending on the product being reviewed. It is useful if one member of the audience is nominated as the chairperson to keep order and resolve conflicts.

The presenter should not feel obliged to defend the product to the bitter end and should be open to valid points. The audience should try to be constructive and not merely critical or personal. The whole atmosphere of the walkthrough should be 'egoless'. That is, it should be approached as a meeting where a group of people try to develop a better product from a prototype that one of them has prepared. It should be clear that it's the product that's being reviewed, not the person or the person's salary.

The main benefit of a structured walkthrough is that a better product is designed. Secondary benefits are that users become more involved in the project and that junior development staff learn from their seniors (even if it is how not to do it).

1.3 CASE tools

In recent years, many software tools have been developed to support structured methods. It is important to realize that the method is the most important thing and the software tool is there to support the method. The general name for these tools is computer aided software engineering (or CASE) tools. However, this could apply to tools used anywhere in the life cycle and a more precise name for tools to support the systems analyst is analyst workbenches.

Most of the techniques that have been mentioned are supported to a greater or lesser extent by analyst workbenches. The use of a good analyst workbench has many advantages over pencil and paper. These might be summarized as the 'word processor' and the 'quality' advantages.

The word processor advantages are that, even though initial diagrams cannot be drawn much more speedily, changes can be made to diagrams quickly and easily without redrawing the whole thing. Also, the diagrams are neater and can be ported to word processing and desktop publishing packages.

The quality advantages are more important and concern the checking and promotion of the various techniques. Using an analyst workbench, the rules of a technique can be checked interactively as it is being used. Also, batch checks can be done for consistency and completeness. In some areas the analyst workbench can actually promote good practice by suggesting a set of allowable objects for the analyst to select or use. A good example of this is when exploding DFDs. When exploding a process, the workbench can automatically take the connected flows and objects to the lower level to be connected to the child diagram. Many (Griffiths and Lockyer, 1992) of the diagrams in this book were originally produced for a series of videos using the CASE tool ASCENT (Lockyer and Griffiths, 1985–97), developed at the University of Teesside.

1.4 Summary

In this introduction, we've looked at the history of structured methods and seen why and how the various techniques evolved over time. We've seen how systems development grew from a creative, uncontrolled activity towards an engineering discipline. First, the programming phase of the life cycle was addressed and structured programming was developed. Then the structured approach was applied to earlier phases of the life cycle. Structure charts were developed to support the systems design phase and data flow diagrams to support the systems analysis phase. This resulted in several first-generation structured systems analysis methods (notably the Yourdon method) that used several of the techniques that had been developed, together with a data dictionary. These methods were essentially process oriented.

Research and development resulted in a second generation of methods where the perspectives on systems development provided by data and behaviour were given more weight. This resulted in new techniques, particularly entity relationship diagrams and entity life histories. Another outcome of this was a new crop of methods, notably SSADM and a new version of the Yourdon method.

Structured methods have been applied to information systems and real-time systems, but in this book we are interested only in information systems.

1.5 Preview

To conclude this introduction, let's see what's to come in the rest of the book. In Chapters 2, 3 and 4 we'll take a detailed look at DFDs. In Chapters 5 and 6, we'll see how to develop the data parts and the process parts of a data dictionary. In Chapter 7, we'll look at how to model data using entity relationship diagrams and data normalization. In Chapter 8, we'll look at how to model the behavioural perspective using entity life histories and take a brief look at state transition diagrams. In Chapter 9, we'll consider the use of structure charts at the systems design stage. Finally, in Chapter 10, we'll consider how the techniques fit together and how they are used in two popular methods: Yourdon and SSADM.

Each chapter (except the last) will have a similar format. First, we'll introduce the theory or notation for a particular technique. Then we'll walk through an example of its use before introducing a problem for you to work. A possible solution will be walked through in the Appendix. As we go through the techniques, we'll be concentrating on their application, based on practical experience. Probably the points where you'll learn the most are not where you're thinking about the theory but when you're actually doing the problems. It will be even better if there are several of you working on this together and you can do some structured walkthroughs.

CHAPTER 2

Introduction to data flow diagrams

2.1 Introduction

In the next three chapters we're going to look at data flow diagrams, or DFDs. The topics that we'll be covering are:

- Drawing conventions
- Current logical models
- Required logical models
- Levelled DFDs and
- DFD styles.

In this chapter we'll be looking at the first two of these.

2.2 DFDs

Data flow diagrams are crucial to many systems analysis methods because a lot of the other techniques depend on them. Their use is helpful to the systems analyst in three main ways: first, they help to structure the mass of information which the analyst discovers; second, they provide an excellent means of communicating with the users of the system; and finally, they allow the system to be modelled at a logical rather than a physical level. That is, we want to get at the logic of the system without the physical detail getting in the way. For example, we may be interested in the fact that invoices are raised, but we're not interested in who in Accounts does this (or even if it is done in Accounts at all).

One reason for this is that the process may well be carried out by computer in the future, so the current location becomes irrelevant. Some methods, like SSADM, do allow locations to be recorded. This can be helpful shorthand when carrying out the initial investigation of the current system and queries need to be resolved, but eventually all models need to be logical.

DFDs show the flow of data around a system, but not the flow of materials. This is because we want to model an information system, and computers can process data but not materials. For example, a computer system can print a shipping note to accompany the delivery of some goods to a customer, but it can't deliver the actual goods.

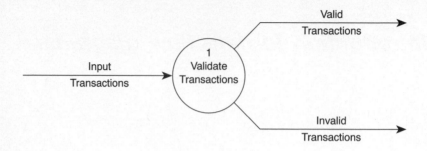

Figure 2.1

Unlike flowcharts, DFDs should not show the flow of control explicitly. That is, there are no decisions and no loops to be seen on the diagrams. These are hidden within the process logic of individual processes, although we can see the data flows that result from decisions. For example, in Figure 2.1, we can see a flow of input transactions going into a process to validate transactions. Inside the process, decisions are taken about the transactions' validity and then two flows emerge – one of valid transactions and one of invalid transactions. But we're getting ahead of ourselves now and should look first at the basic drawing conventions.

DFDs are a network representation of a system using just four symbols. The initial notation that we are using comes from the Yourdon method, but we will look at other notations later.

The first symbol is the external entity (sometimes called a terminator). It is drawn on a diagram as a named square, as in Figure 2.2. These symbols are used for things outside the system. They may be outside the company completely (e.g. customers), or they may be just other departments in the company not affected by the development (e.g. a sales department). Another common external entity is a computer system that's the source or destination of some data, e.g. an accounts package. Each external entity is usually identified by a lower-case letter. Sometimes (to avoid crossing lines on the diagram) entities are duplicated. If this is necessary, an angled line is put in the corner of the box.

The second symbol is the process. It is shown on the diagram as a named circle, as in Figure 2.3. Each process is identified by a number, and has a

Figure 2.2

Figure 2.3

description of the action or transformation taking place. The description should be an imperative statement consisting of an active verb and object; for example, 'Check credit worthiness', 'Print sales report'. Because of the size of the symbol, the description must obviously be very short. Vague verbs like 'process' or 'handle' may indicate a lack of understanding on the part of the analyst. Alternatively, they may be a valid way of summarizing a lot of detail.

Notice that the statements have no subjects: that is, we don't say who carries out the process or where. This helps our logical view of the system.

The third symbol is the data flow. These are shown as named arrows, as in Figure 2.4. The name of the data flow should be the name of the data object passing between the two connected symbols. Two-way flows of data may be shown and some methods recommend the use of two flow names in these cases.

The last of the four symbols is the data store. These are represented as named parallel lines, as in Figure 2.5. The data in a data store is data at rest (or persistent data), rather like master files or databases. This contrasts with the data in data flows, which is data in motion, rather like transactions.

Each data store is identified by a name. A useful convention is to use the plural for store names and the singular for flow names. Some methods also recommend numbering stores.

If data stores need to be duplicated for diagram neatness, a vertical line should be added to the left of both copies. When data is written to a data store,

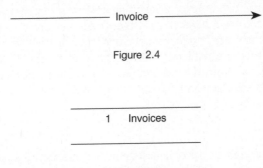

Figure 2.4

Figure 2.5

the data flow is shown going in. When data is read from a data store, the data flow is shown coming out. If data is being read and stored, we can use the double-headed arrow.

Note that all data flows must involve a process at one or both ends (apart from in one or two special circumstances that we will describe later). This is because processes are the dynamic parts of the system which cause data to flow. They are the forces that pull and push the data around the model. External entities and data stores are static and they have no force to move the data, so it's incorrect to join them directly.

Also, self-linking is not allowed and all processes must have input and output flows. There is no point in a process that has only input data flows. If the data is not stored, or transformed and moved to another process or external entity, there is no point in modelling it. Often, though, one of these actions will be happening and it has just been left out of the model. Similarly, it is impossible to have a process with only output data flows. If it has no data on which to work it has nothing to transform or move.

An external entity may have only output flows (if it is just a source of data), only input flows (it is just a destination for data), or both input and output flows (if it is a source and destination).

Data stores should usually have both input and output data flows. A data store with only input data flows implies that the data is being stored for nothing. A data store with only output data flows has no visible means of creating or amending its data. In both cases, this might be allowable if the data store is used or created and maintained in another computer system. However, it could be argued that an external entity would be a better representation in this case.

EXAMPLE 2.1

A college processes applications for its postgraduate courses from home graduates and those from other institutions. The admissions section records the date of receipt of all applications in the applications book. Home graduates are accepted if they meet the entry requirements (this is also checked against lists of previous examination results by the records section). Other graduates are rejected if they don't meet the entry requirements, and even if they do, a reference is sought. If this is satisfactory, the graduate is accepted. All applicants receive a letter from the college advising them if they've been accepted or rejected, and the date that this is sent is recorded in the applications book.

SOLUTION

Let's go through this problem statement sentence by sentence, and think about how a DFD could be built up.

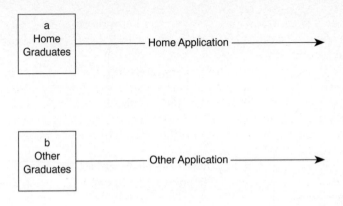

Figure 2.6

The first sentence says 'A college processes applications for postgraduate courses from home graduates, and those from other institutions'. From reading the problem statement once we know that the first half of the sentence is a general description of the whole system and can therefore be largely ignored. However, it does give us the major input to the system, 'application'. The second half of the sentence gives us the sources, 'home graduates' and 'other graduates'. So, we might start our DFD as in Figures 2.6 or 2.7. There's not much to choose between these options, but for simplicity we'll continue with the second.

The next sentence says 'The admissions section records the date of receipt of all applications in the applications book'. This details a process that we might describe as 'Record Application' and add to our diagram as in Figure 2.8. The applications book is a permanent record of all applications, and is therefore a data store. The data that flows from the process to the data store is the date of receipt of the applications.

Notice how the description of the process is phrased as an imperative statement with an active verb and object. Notice also that the subject (the admissions section) doesn't appear on the diagram at all. It's not an external entity because it's not outside the system. It's merely the place where the process is carried out. As we said when

Figure 2.7

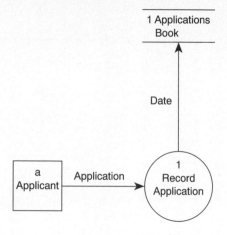

Figure 2.8

we were looking at the drawing conventions for processes, we're not interested in the places where these are carried out or the people that do them. This is because the processes may well be performed on a computer in the future. We want to get at the real processes in the system without any of the physical detail clouding the picture.

The next sentence tells us 'Home graduates are accepted if they meet the entry requirements (this is also checked against lists of previous examination results by the records section)'. This gives us another process which we could describe as 'Check Entry Requirements' (see Figure 2.9).

Notice once more the phrasing of the process description. Also notice the absence of the records section from the diagram, which again is just the place where the process is carried out.

The process must have access to two data stores to allow checks to be done: a store of the entry requirements for each course and lists of previous examination results. We're not told at this point what happens on acceptance or rejection, so we'll leave that until later.

The next two sentences say 'Other graduates are rejected if they don't meet the entry requirements, and even if they do, a reference is sought. If this is satisfactory, the graduate is accepted.'

The first part of this ('Checking Entry Requirements') is the same as for home graduates. However, it's obvious that we can't use the process that we've just drawn for 'other graduates' too. The reason for this is that it not only checks entry requirements, but also checks against lists of previous examination results. While it might be imagined that these could exist for home graduates, it's hard to believe that there's such a store of data that we could call on for all other

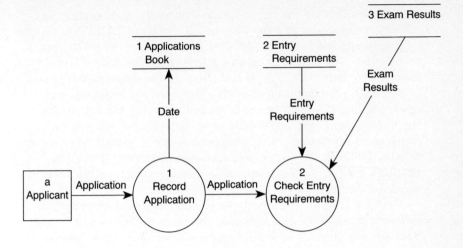

Figure 2.9

graduates as well! Therefore the diagram must be changed to look like Figure 2.10. Now, all applications may go through the basic entry requirements check, but after that the home applications only go to be checked against lists of previous examination results.

Similarly, only other applications are referred for a reference. This process wouldn't access a store of references because it's difficult to

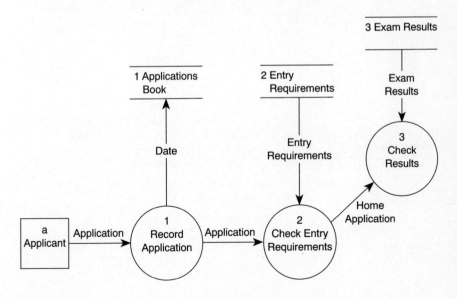

Figure 2.10

imagine one existing for all graduates. Rather, an external entity (a referee) is introduced into the diagram, as in Figure 2.11.

Finally, the last two sentences describe what happens on acceptance or rejection. 'All applicants receive a letter from the college advising them if they have been accepted or rejected. The date that this is sent is recorded in the applications book.' There are two processes here again: sending letters to the applicant and recording the date in the applications book. We could draw these as processes, but it's not really necessary because what's happening here is trivial. When we are drawing DFDs, if we do no more than recognize every process and faithfully draft it, we'll end up with a diagram where we can't see the wood for the trees!

The trick is in the intelligent combination of processes so that sufficient detail is presented without obscuring the big picture. Yourdon recommends an ideal diagram size of about seven processes, because this has been shown to be the amount of detail that people can cope with. One of the most fruitful areas for economizing on processes is when looking at 'output' processes; that is, processes that

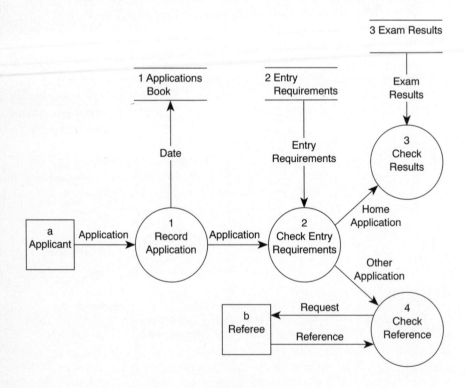

Figure 2.11

are just sending information to a store or external. So here we might just draw letters going straight out of the system from the checking processes to the original external entity, the applicant, as in Figure 2.12. This may be duplicated on the right of the diagram for neatness. The storing of the date in the applications book may be drawn similarly.

We must also return to 'Check Entry Requirements', the other point on the diagram where rejection could have occurred. We add the letter to the applicant and the date to the application book, as in Figure 2.13.

Stores that are linked only to one process, like the Entry Requirements store, may be omitted because they can be considered to be local to the process; that is, implicitly part of the process that's being carried out. This is sometimes useful with a busy diagram, but if this isn't the case, it's better to show as much as possible for completeness. This will make for more effective communication with the user.

Notice that the 'Entry Requirements' and 'Exam Results' data stores break the rules that were proposed earlier in the chapter in that they have an output and no input. This will be followed up in the next chapter.

Sometimes when we've finished a DFD we need to combine processes because the diagram has grown too large. Yourdon suggests that the number of processes on a diagram should be no more than about seven, based on earlier psychological research. In this case we could combine 'Record Application' with 'Check Entry Requirements'. However, as there are only four processes, and this is well within the limits proposed by Yourdon, there is no need.

In Exercise 2.1 below, read through the problem statement and try building up a DFD as we've just done in the example. Some people find it helpful to make lists of the processes, stores, externals and flows before sketching the diagram. You might try this to see if you find it useful.

Exercise 2.1

When a request is received from a customer, the sales office raises an order. Orders are passed to the credit control department where the customer's credit worthiness is checked. If credit approval is not granted, the order is referred back to the sales office for the attention of the sales manager. If the order is accepted, it is passed to the stock office where the availability of each item on the order is checked by the stock clerk. If all the items on the

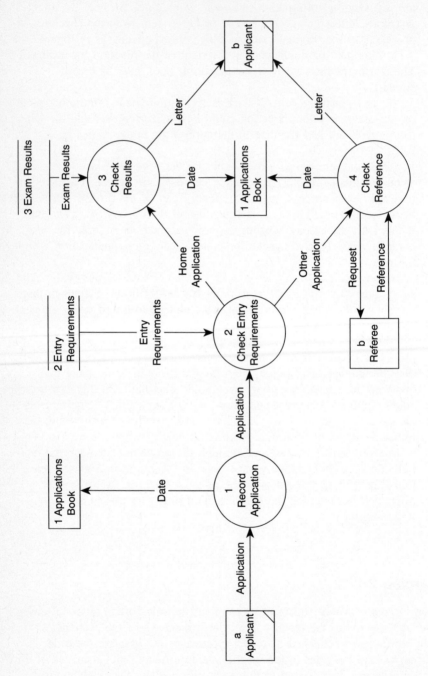

Figure 2.12

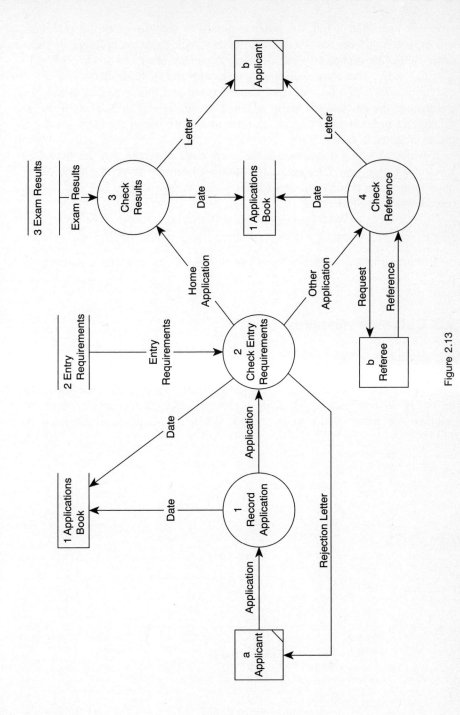

Figure 2.13

order are available in full, the order is passed to the warehouse for picking and despatch and the stock clerk adjusts the stock cards accordingly. If the order cannot be completely satisfied out of current stock the stock clerk will split the order. The clerk will raise a part-order out of those items and quantities which **can** be met from current stock and this is passed to the warehouse, the stock-cards being adjusted accordingly. The balance of the customer's order is used to raise another part-order which the stock clerk places in a 'back orders file'.

If while adjusting a stock-card, the stock clerk observes that the stock level of an item now falls below the stipulated reorder level, the stock clerk must inform the purchasing department which is now responsible for replenishing the stock.

Draw a DFD to model this system.

A solution to this exercise is walked through in the Appendix, starting on p. 175.

2.3 Common mistakes

It is instructive to highlight some common mistakes made when drawing DFDs. One is the use of processes as places. Sometimes this is obvious, as in Figure 2.14. However, sometimes it's more subtle, as in Figure 2.15. Here the DFD looks OK at first glance, but then it seems strange that rejected orders are returned for more orders to be raised. When the diagram is inspected in

Figure 2.14

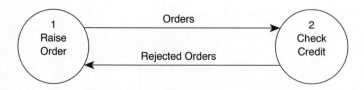

Figure 2.15

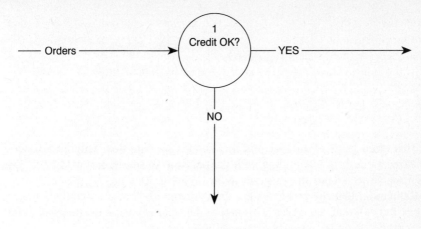

Figure 2.16

conjunction with the narrative, it's obvious that the rejected orders are being returned not to the process but to the place where the process is being carried out (the sales office).

Another common mistake is showing decisions explicitly. Consider the fragment of DFD in Figure 2.16. What this actually means on a DFD is that we are trying to credit something called an 'OK'. Two flows emerge, one comprising things called 'Yes's', and one things called 'No's'. This is obviously nonsense, and should be drawn as in Figure 2.17.

Showing material flow is another common mistake. There's often the temptation to 'finish off' a diagram with material flow. For example, in an ordering system, one of the net outputs from the system might be a flow of order details to the warehouse as in Figure 2.18. It might be tempting to replace the warehouse with the fragment of DFD in Figure 2.19. This is unnecessary because our computer system will never be able to deliver goods to the customer, so there's little point in modelling it.

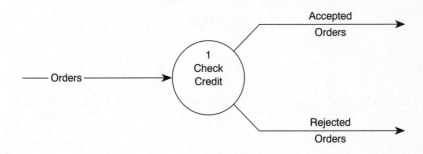

Figure 2.17

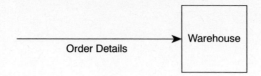

Figure 2.18

This often leads to another mistake, showing a data flow without a process on at least one end. Continuing with the previous example, it would have been even worse to extend the diagram as in Figure 2.20.

Remember that the processes are the dynamic parts of the diagram, and the stores and externals are static. This means data can't flow on the diagram unless it's pushed or pulled by a process.

Finally, it's unnecessary to constantly use intermediate files on the diagram (see Figure 2.21). This tends to complicate the picture and obscure the important points, particularly which are the real data stores.

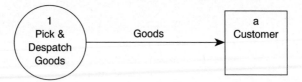

Figure 2.19

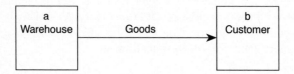

Figure 2.20

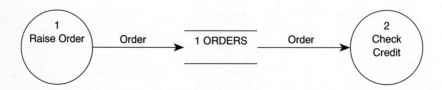

Figure 2.21

2.4 Summary

It's useful now to summarize the important points that we've learnt about drawing DFDs:

- The DFD should be built up from close inspection of the problem statement, or lists that have been made from the problem statement. In a real situation this is likely to be interview notes.
- Processes may need to be combined to give diagrams of an understandable size. Also, trivial processes should be merged with others to avoid cluttering the diagram with unimportant detail. Prime candidates for this are 'output' processes.
- Naming is very important, particularly for flows and processes. Flows should be named as precisely as possible to help communication. Processes should be described as an imperative statement consisting of an active verb and object with no subject. The subject is unlikely to appear on the diagram at all to help our logical view of the system.
- It may be necessary to 'invent' data stores to allow the operation of some processes, particularly checking. If these stores are used by only one process they may be hidden inside it if the diagram is full.
- External entities may be used on a diagram as a 'black box' for things that we would like to model but for which we don't yet have the necessary information.

CHAPTER 3

Progressing data flow diagrams

3.1 Introduction

In the previous chapter we saw how to develop what are known as current logical DFDs. That is, the diagram shows a model of the system as it currently operates in essence, or logically, with no reference to its physical environment. In this chapter we'll look at how to develop required logical DFDs.

3.2 Required logical DFDs

Current logical DFDs show us the underlying logic of a system as it currently operates. This is useful in the early stages of development to help the analyst understand the problem domain and to involve the user. However, it is important that the analyst does not dwell too long on the current system, but moves on to consider what is required in the future, i.e. the required system. This is modelled using a required logical DFD.

For any required logical model there will probably be several alternative physical implementations. For example, we might have constructed a current logical model of a branch ordering system that uses a central warehouse. The current physical implementation might be the branches phoning the warehouse with their orders. In the new system, we would want to consider other alternatives; like installing terminals at the branches, or putting in a point-of-sale network. These options would have to be looked at for technical and economic feasibility. That is, for each option we would have to see if it was technically possible and economically viable. The presentation of these analyses would allow a decision to be made about which option to implement. It's beyond the scope of this chapter to go into cost–benefit analyses and corporate decision making, but we will be looking at the way in which required logical DFDs are constructed.

The required logical DFD is derived from the current logical DFD as follows. The first step is to consider each process in turn to see whether it could (and should) be automated. It's difficult to give much guidance about making these decisions, as they tend to rely on experience. Generally, any process that could be done by computer, and follows definable rules, is a candidate for automation. If we've constructed our current logical DFD correctly and included only data flow and not material flow, most of the processes probably could be carried out on the computer. However, any process that requires some human intelligence or judgement must be ruled out. For example, we couldn't expect the system to check prospective employees' references to see if they were satisfactory.

In addition, we might have experiences of processes that could be automated, but might be better done manually. For example, one supermarket chain paid a substantial five-figure sum for some routing software to work out its branch delivery schedule. There were various trials and the delivery of the software was eagerly awaited. When it arrived and was used, many of the routes that it suggested were clearly ridiculous. Also, it took the routing clerk longer to prepare the input to the package than it used to take him to work out the routes. Its use at the company was continued only to spare the blushes of those who had made the decision to purchase and people were set to work looking for alternative uses of the software.

Once it has been decided which processes on the current logical model to automate, the next step is to enclose them all inside a dotted line. This is known as the automation boundary and encloses the development area. In addition to the processes, stores and flows should appear in the development area if they are to be computerized. However, it would be wrong to include an external entity in the development area. For example, if we included the external entity 'customer', this would mean that we were going to automate our customers, which doesn't make sense.

When the automation boundary has been marked, the final step in the development of the required logical model is to redraw the DFD. To do this we need to consider the parts of the diagram outside and inside the automation boundary separately.

In the part of the diagram outside the automation boundary, we want to get rid of all processes and stores. That is, we want to regress this part of the diagram to external entities. The reason for this is that if the processes and stores are not going to be automated, we've little further interest in them in developing a new computer system. When we've changed this part of the diagram we should have a number of flows crossing the automation boundary going straight to external entities.

Within the development area, there are a number of changes that we should consider. First, if the current system is manual (or partly manual), we need to consider how processes will be different when they are automated. A common change here is the inclusion of data stores linked to data input processes to allow data validation. For example, in Figure 3.1 Customers and Stock stores are being used to validate orders as they are entered.

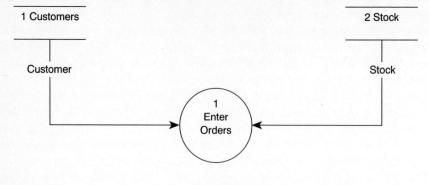

Figure 3.1

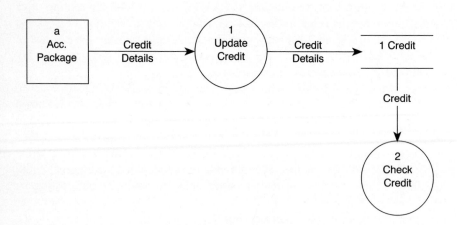

Figure 3.2

Also, there may be extra processes needed. These are often to do with the maintenance of data stores. For example, in Figure 3.2 we can see a process 'Update Credit' that has been added to get information from the accounts package to update the Credit store.

Second, if the current system has problems (and which one hasn't?), consider how the diagram needs to be changed to solve these. Finally, if the users have identified any new requirements (and which ones don't?), consider how the diagram needs to be changed to incorporate these. This will then result in a required logical DFD.

EXAMPLE 3.1

If we look at the current logical DFD in Figure 3.3, we can see that most of the processes could easily be automated. For example, we

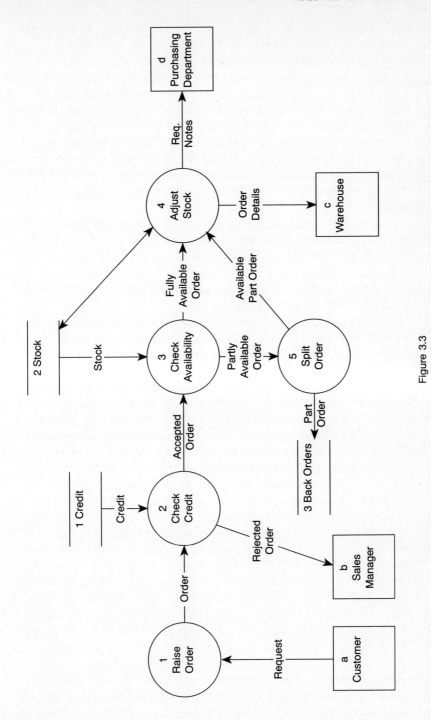

Figure 3.3

could raise an order by typing the details into the system. We could
check availability by comparing the orders to the stock, and so on.

The only possible exception is the 'Check Credit' process. If this is
a simple file check, then it could be automated. However, if it requires
a telephone call, or an assessment of the state of the customer's
business, it couldn't be automated. Here we'll decide to make a simple
file check initially, and produce a report of customers failing the check
for the sales manager to investigate further. This would result in our
diagram being extended as in Figure 3.4. Now the 'Check Credit'
process would be automated, but 'Investigate Rejections' would not.
This would result in an automation boundary on the diagram as
shown.

Notice that only the externals and the 'investigate rejections'
process remain outside the development area. The process should be
removed and replaced with an external entity, say Sales Manager, as
in Figure 3.5. Notice that once this had been done we would no
longer show the flow of rejections back to the customer as this would
break our rules for drawing DFDs.

Now we need to concentrate on the part of the diagram inside the
automation boundary. First, we need to consider the computer
perspective. As we said earlier, the two common areas of change here
are data input and data stores. Here the data input is the flow of
customer requests into the 'Raise Order' process. We might rename
the process 'Enter Orders' to better describe its new function.

Also, when orders are entered into the system, we want to make
sure that the data is as correct as possible to prevent problems later.
That is, we want to prevent 'garbage in, garbage out'. To stop
incorrect data entering the system, extensive validation checks are
carried out. Most of these checks e.g. numeric, range, alphabetic will
not show on the diagram; they are merely part of the internal logic of
the process. However, file checks will show on the DFD in the form
of stores linked to the validation process, as in Figure 3.6. For
example, we might expect the order to contain several item numbers
in the range 1000–2999. The 'Enter Orders' process could check that
item numbers are numeric and in the correct range without extension
to the diagram. But if we were going to check that a particular item
number actually existed on the Stock file, we would have to link the
Stock store to the process (as in Figure 3.6). Notice that now the part
of the diagram outside the development area has been dealt with there
is no longer any need to show the automation boundary.

We also need to consider the data stores. The 'Credit' store will
become a computer file because it's in the development area, but it
won't appear by magic! We need to show a process that's capable of

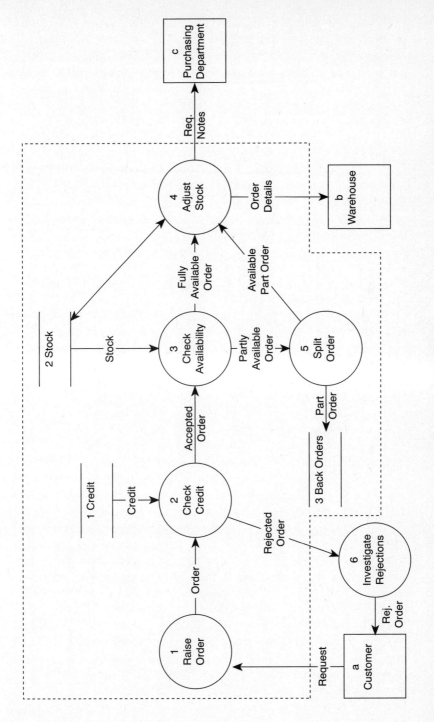

Figure 3.4

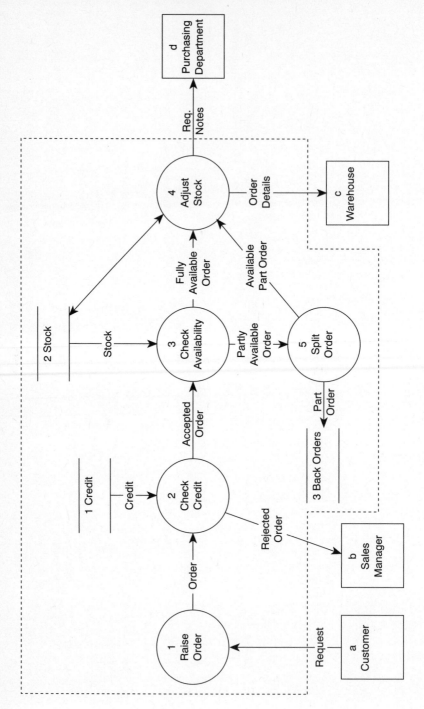

Figure 3.5

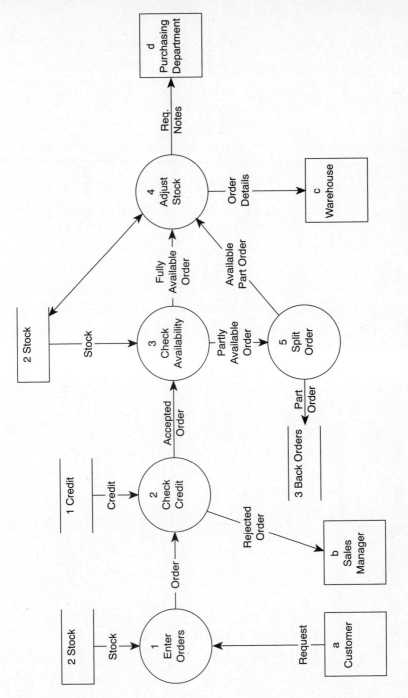

Figure 3.6

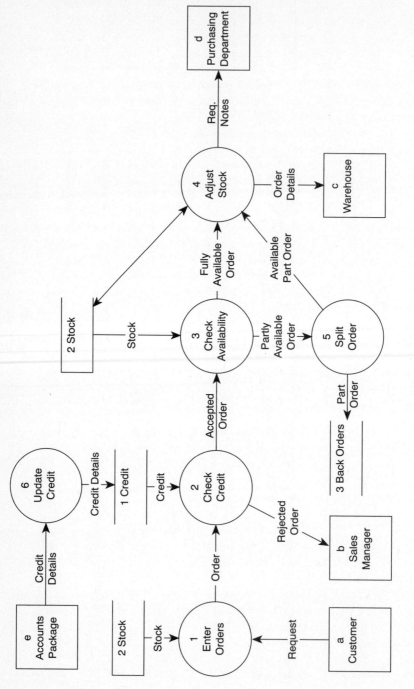

Figure 3.7

creating and changing the store (and we need to show its source). This might extend our diagram as in Figure 3.7.

The Stock store appears not to need any further work at first because it's being read from and written to. But when we think about it a bit more, it's obvious that stock levels are only ever being adjusted downwards. Therefore, we need to add something to our diagram that will adjust them upwards. This might result in an extension as in Figure 3.8.

The 'Back Orders' store has problems because it's only being written to. This means that it will just continue to grow. Obviously, we need some way of feeding back orders back into the system to see if they can be cleared. This could be done with an extra flow as in Figure 3.9.

We also need to consider potential problems with the diagram. For example, back orders may be on file for some time. Over this period the customer's credit rating might deteriorate. Therefore, it might make sense not only to check availability for back orders, but also to recheck credit. This can be done by linking the back orders not to 'Check Availability' as we have it now, but right back to 'Check Credit', as in Figure 3.10.

Finally, we need to incorporate new requirements. In this system, the warehouse manager might request a weekly report of back orders more than two weeks old. This could be added as in Figure 3.11.

Notice that we are now up to Yourdon's limit of about seven processes per diagram. If this diagram was going to get much bigger it would need to be 'exploded', which we will look at in the next chapter.

In Exercise 3.1 below, go through the same steps that we have just been through in the example to build up a required logical model.

Exercise 3.1

An oil company has two road distribution terminals on Teesside – one at North Tees and one at South Bank. All 'office work' is carried out at the North Tees site.

Orders are received from customers by telephone and noted on a despatch note (DN). These details are extended from a customer card index and filed by requested delivery date.

The day before despatch, orders are routed. The South Bank terminal is advised by telephone of orders to be despatched from there the following day. At North Tees, DNs are passed to the despatch clerk who places them in pigeonholes by vehicle. The next day these are given to drivers when

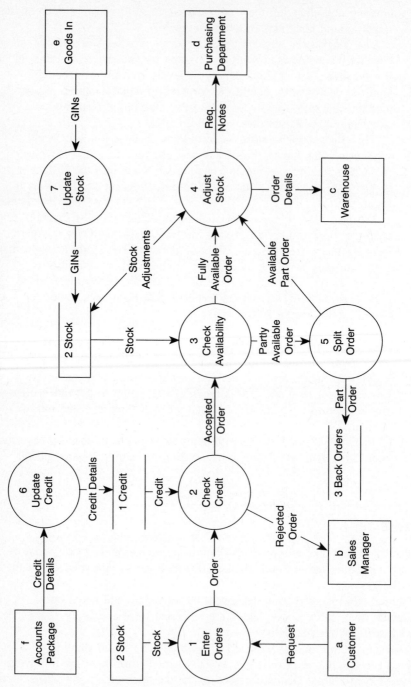

Figure 3.8

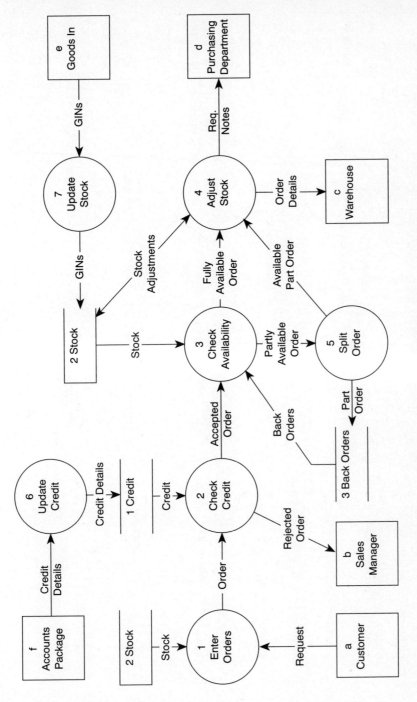

Figure 3.9

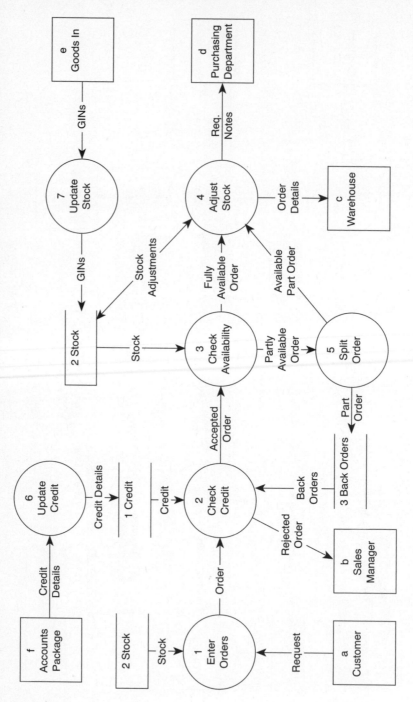

Figure 3.10

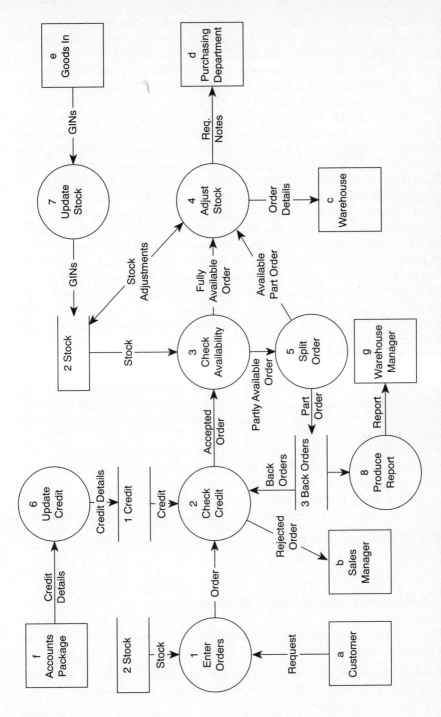

Figure 3.11

they arrive. The drivers stamp the DN at the pump when loading to show the quantity loaded. They then deliver the product and obtain a signature on the DN from the recipient. The day after delivery, South Bank telephones the North Tees office to advise details of quantities delivered. At North Tees, the despatch clerk receives the previous day's DNs from the drivers as they arrive and passes them to the office.

In the office, DN details for customers in the private sector are entered at a PC. These are then transmitted to head office where invoices are produced and sent to customers. All aspects of payment are dealt with at head office.

For public sector customers, North Tees maintains records of quantities delivered and sends out invoices at month-end. Note that the company despatches a number of different products, each with a different selling price. Again, all aspects of payment are dealt with by head office.

Duty is paid to Customs and Excise at the end of each month by North Tees for product delivered to both public and private sector customers. To this end, details of totals delivered by product are maintained (for both terminals). At month-end, a cheque is sent to Customs together with a statement giving the breakdown by product. Duty is levied at different rates for different products.

A current logical DFD of this system, with automation boundary marked, is presented as Figure 3.12.

One problem with the system is names and addresses being out of date on invoices for public sector customers. This is because the information is put on to the delivery note at the time of the original order and by the time delivery has been made and an invoice raised, two months could have passed. This makes for delays in payment which management are obviously unhappy about.

A new requirement from head office is that they want to receive a monthly summary by product of the amount invoiced (for public sector customers) and the amount paid in duty (for all customers).

Draw a required logical DFD to model the new system.

A solution to this exercise is walked through in the Appendix, starting on p. 183.

3.3 Required logical DFD summary

Now, before we go on to look at levelling DFDs, it's useful to summarize what we have learnt about drawing required logical DFDs:

• First, we inspect each process on the current logical DFD and decide if it should be automated. This gives rise to an automation boundary enclosing a development area.

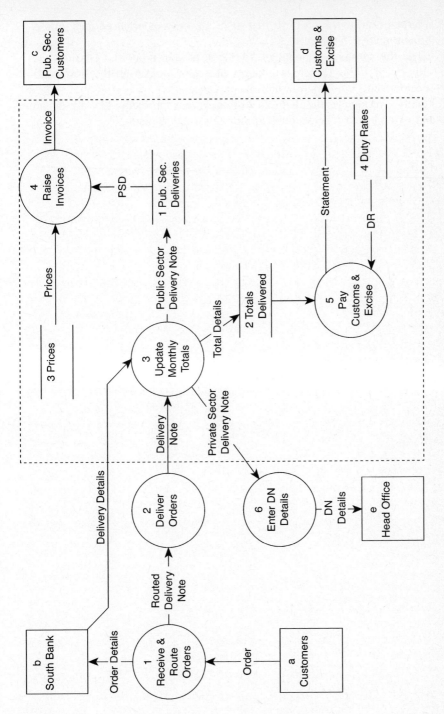

Figure 3.12

- We then redraw the DFD so that there are only external entities outside the automation boundary.
- Inside the automation boundary, we look at data input and consider the addition of stores to help validation. We then look at all the stores and consider their combination and maintenance.
- Finally, we change the diagram to remove any problems that are apparent and extend it to take account of any new requirements.

CHAPTER 4

Exploding DFDs

4.1 Introduction

In this chapter we're going to look at exploding, or levelling, DFDs and the different ways of going about drawing them proposed by various structured systems analysis methods.

4.2 Explosion

So far we've modelled a system using just a single diagram. This is fine for small systems, or in the early stages of a development, but if we're going to stick to our rule of about seven processes per diagram we need a way of providing more detail. This is done by exploding the processes on the diagram.

The top-level DFD is developed as before. This represents the highest level of abstraction of the model. Each process is examined to see if it would usefully split into sub-processes. If it would, a lower-level DFD is developed to model just that process.

The processes of the child diagram could then be exploded in the same way if necessary. It's difficult to say precisely how far explosion should be taken. Although we shouldn't be thinking about implementation while we're developing a logical model, we might consider this in programming terms. Explosion should certainly be applied where a process is larger than a discrete program. Usually, it should be continued until each process is about the size of a procedure or section of a program, but not further than this.

When exploding processes, decimal numbering is used. That is, process 4 explodes to 4.1, 4.2, etc.; then 4.1 explodes to 4.1.1 and 4.1.2, and so on.

It's common to show the child diagram within the parent process, as in Figure 4.1. The objects connected at the upper level are arranged around the edge and are joined to individual objects on the lower-level diagram. This clearly shows the boundary between the levels. The objects from the parent diagram are often shown dotted by software tools, which further reinforces this.

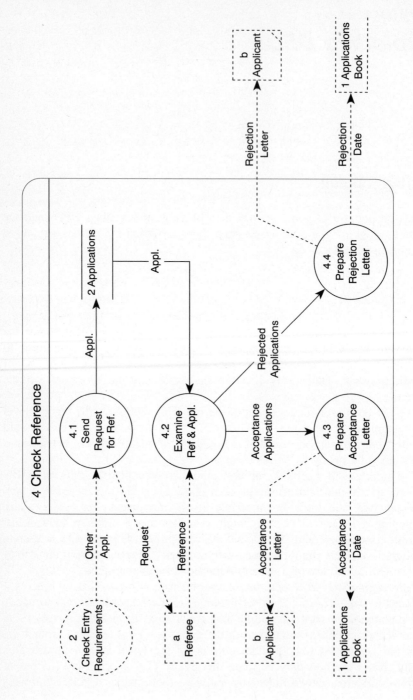

Figure 4.1

When processes are exploded, it's allowable to use new data stores that were not on the upper-level diagram. As long as these are local to the process, there's no need to add them to the parent diagram. Alternatively, if a new external entity is needed on the explosion, it is generally regarded as being an omission from the parent diagram, and it's usually drawn there instead.

A levelled set of DFDs is said to be 'balanced' if the net inputs and outputs of the child diagrams correspond to the inputs and outputs of the relevant parent processes. On a simple level, if there's a flow in and a flow out of the parent process; there should be a flow in and a flow out of the child diagram. However, as long as the net inputs and outputs of the parent process and the child diagram are logically equivalent, there's no need to maintain a strict one-to-one correspondence.

For example, there might be a flow of 'shipping details' emerging from the parent process (see process 1 on Figure 4.2). At the lower level, there might be two flows emerging from the child diagram, say 'despatch note' and 'invoice', that together make up 'shipping details' (see Figure 4.3). In this case, while the DFD set is numerically unbalanced, it is logically balanced.

This is a good illustration of hierarchical, top-down modelling. The top-level diagram is the most abstract representation of the whole system and the explosions are progressively more precise models of parts of the system. Within the model we have notions not only of decomposing processes, but also of decomposing data. That is, as we go down the model, processes may be expressed in terms of sub-processes and flows in terms of sub-flows.

To help you understand balancing, and demonstrate how explosion is carried out, let's look at an example.

EXAMPLE 4.1

If we think back to the diagram developed in Example 2.1, let us consider exploding 'Check Reference' shown in Figure 4.4. There are two flows going into the process, and three coming out. These must all be tied in to our lower-level diagram in some way.

On further investigation, we might discover that the process is made up of four steps. The first step is to send a request for a reference to the referee and file the application. This could be drawn as a process 'Send Request for Reference', with a flow of 'Applications' going to a store, as in Figure 4.5. The store wasn't shown on the upper-level diagram, but as it's local to the process there's no need to add it there. The input to the process would be 'Other Application' from the upper level. Also, there would be another output from the process, 'Request', going to the upper level.

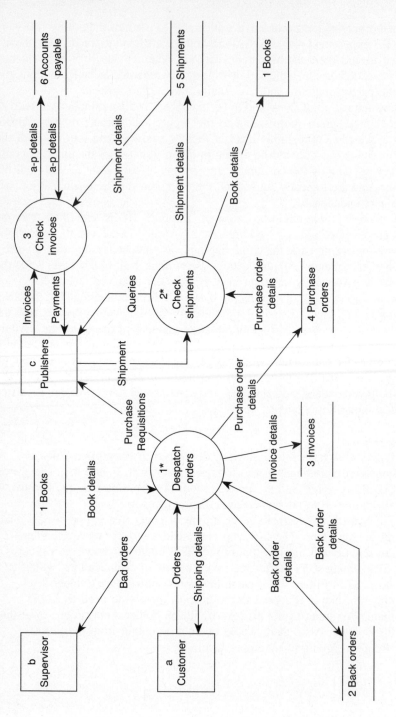

Figure 4.2

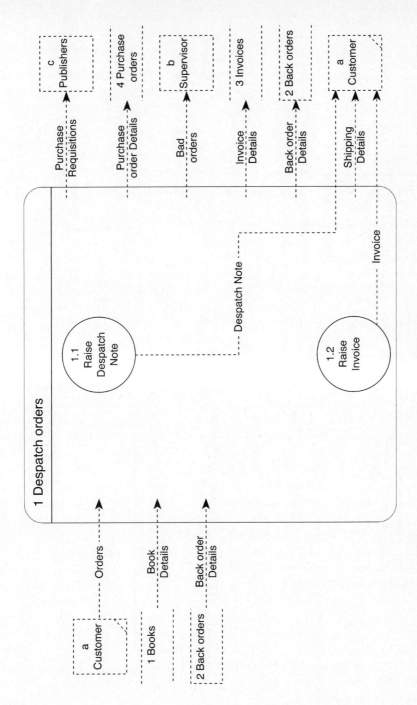

Figure 4.3

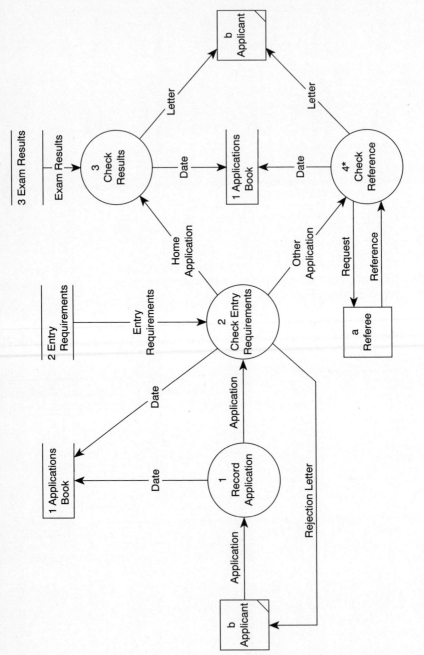

Figure 4.4

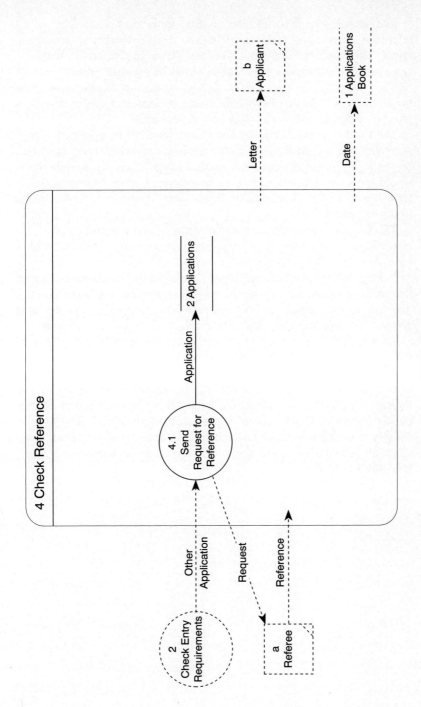

Figure 4.5

The second step is to find the original application when the reference arrives, and to examine both to decide whether to accept or reject. This could be drawn as a process 'Examine Reference and Application' (see Figure 4.6). There would be an input flow 'Reference' from the upper level, and an input flow 'Application' from the local store. The process would create two internal output flows: 'Accepted Application' and 'Rejected Application'.

The third step is to send an acceptance letter if the application is accepted, and record the date in the applications book. This could be drawn as a process 'Prepare Acceptance Letter' (see Figure 4.7). It would have two outputs connected to the upper level: 'Acceptance Date' going to the 'Applications Book', and 'Acceptance Letter' going to the 'Applicant'.

The last step is to send a rejection letter if the application is rejected, and record the date in the applications book. This could be modelled similarly to the previous step, as in Figure 4.8.

Notice that the diagram set is now numerically unbalanced. That is, the parent process has two inputs and three outputs, while the child diagram has two inputs and five outputs. The difference is in the letter going to the applicant and the date going to the applications book.

On the top-level diagram, we had 'letter' going to applicant, but on the explosion we've distinguished between acceptance and rejection letters. We could combine processes 4.3 and 4.4 to avoid this. There is no need, though, because 'letter' on the top-level diagram is logically equivalent to 'acceptance letter' plus 'rejection letter' on the child diagram. It's just that the explosion is more precise, which is entirely consistent with the concept of data decomposition. Therefore, although at first sight the diagram set appears to be unbalanced, it is logically balanced.

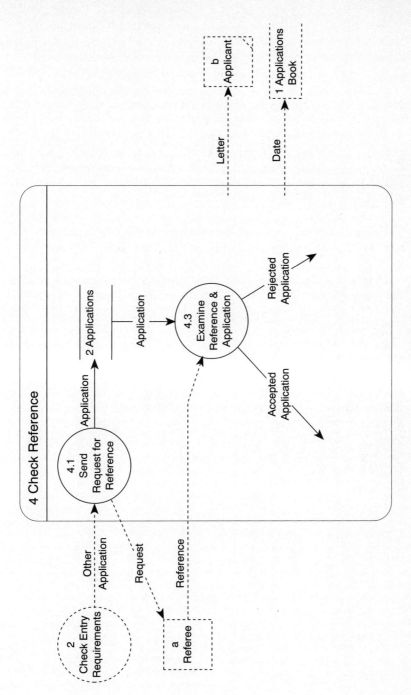

Figure 4.6

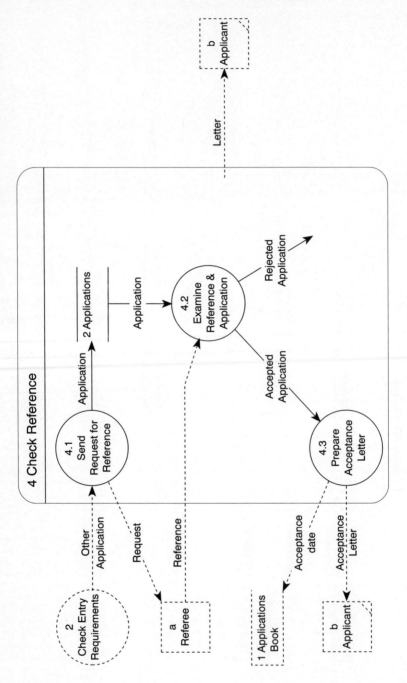

4 Check Reference

4.1 Send Request for Reference

2 Applications

Application

4.2 Examine Reference & Application

Rejected Application

Accepted Application

4.3 Prepare Acceptance Letter

2 Check Entry Requirements

Other Application

Request

Reference

a Referee

Acceptance date

1 Applications Book

Acceptance Letter

b Applicant

Letter

b Applicant

Figure 4.7

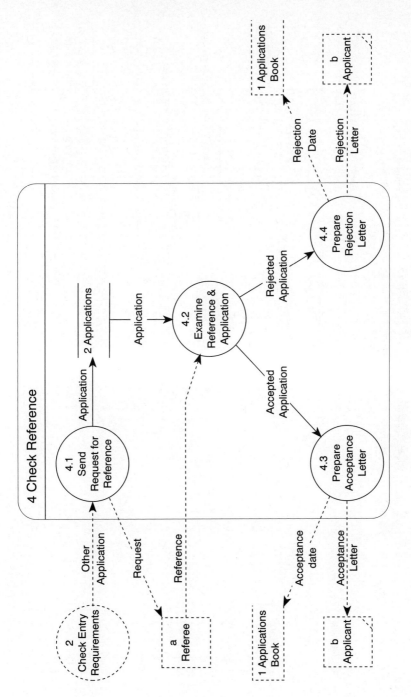

Figure 4.8

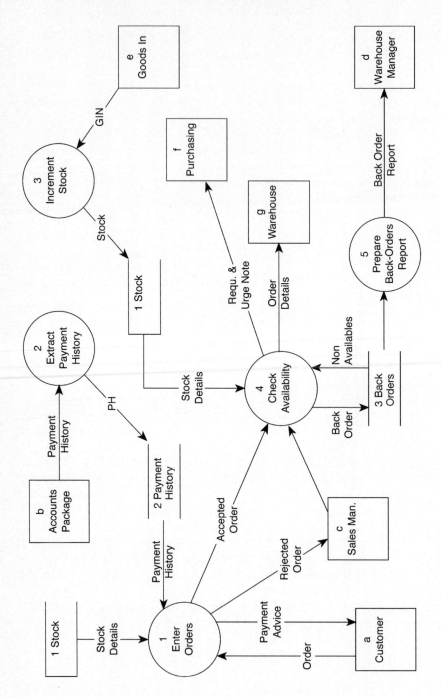

Figure 4.9

Exercise 4.1

In Figure 4.9 process 1, Enter Orders, is to be exploded. The process is described below in detail.

Orders from customers comprise order details and, optionally, payment. Order details are checked for valid stock numbers. Orders failing this check are referred to the sales manager.

For cash sales, payments are checked against prices on the stock file. One of two 'payment advices' might be sent to the customer. Overpayments result in a credit being sent. Underpayments result in a payment request being sent, and the order is held awaiting correct payment. When the payment is correct, the order continues through the system.

For credit sales, credit status is checked by inspecting the payment history file. Rejected orders are referred to the sales manager.

Explode process 1, Enter Orders, to a lower-level diagram.

A solution to this exercise is walked through in the Appendix, starting on p. 194.

4.3 DFD styles

Before we leave the topic of DFDs, we'll take a look at the different styles of drawing them in different structured systems analysis methods, in particular Yourdon and SSADM.

One obvious difference is the notation. For example, the diagram in Figure 4.10 drawn in Yourdon notation would look like Figure 4.11 in SSADM notation.

The differences are mainly cosmetic, but there are some more important variations. For completeness, dotted flows can be drawn on SSADM DFDs between terminators. Also, locations are included for the processes. This is a small sign of an important difference in philosophy concerning the approach that the two methods propose for the development of DFDs.

SSADM states that the final DFD set is arrived at by proceeding through a series of models. In the previous chapter we saw how we could first draw a current logical DFD and then transform it into a required logical DFD. SSADM goes further than this and proposes a series of three models: current physical, current logical and required logical. The locations recorded for SSADM processes are used only in the current physical model.

4.4 Event partitioning

Yourdon, on the other hand, recommends the use of only one model: the essential model. This corresponds to the required logical model, but is arrived

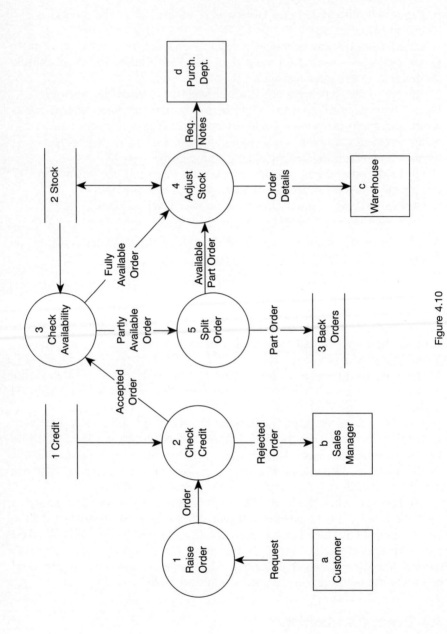

Figure 4.10

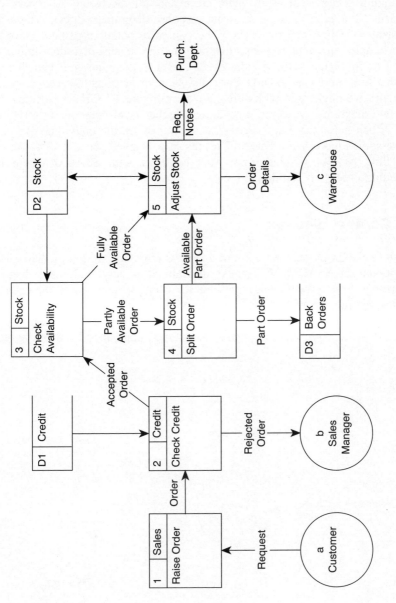

Figure 4.11

at by a completely different process called event partitioning. First, all the events, or external stimuli, of the system are identified. For example, we might be looking at a system where there are events for the receipt of orders and payments. For each of these an event response diagram is drawn. These are fragments of DFDs that model how the system responds to particular events. For example, an event response diagram for the receipt of orders might be drawn as in Figure 4.12. All the event response diagrams are then merged together to form one large DFD. For example, after merging the event response diagrams, we might start with a diagram as in Figure 4.13. If we partition this into two diagrams, we could then draw a higher-level diagram, as in Figure 4.14. When these processes are exploded, we can see the individual diagrams below as in Figure 4.15. This still results in a levelled set of DFDs, but the modelling process is bottom-up. This contrasts with SSADM where the modelling process is top-down.

4.5 Context diagram

Yourdon also proposes the notion of a context diagram (see Figure 4.16). This is optional in SSADM. A context diagram is a very high-level diagram consisting of one process that represents the whole system and all the external entities that interact with it. The purpose of such a diagram is to show clearly all a system's interfaces with its environment. No stores should appear on this diagram, apart from 'external' stores, i.e. stores maintained by other systems

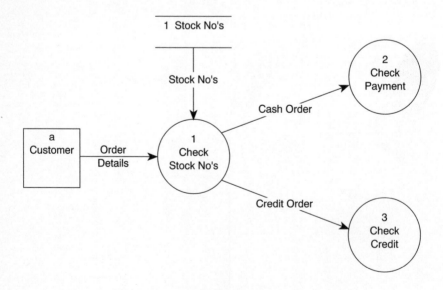

Figure 4.12

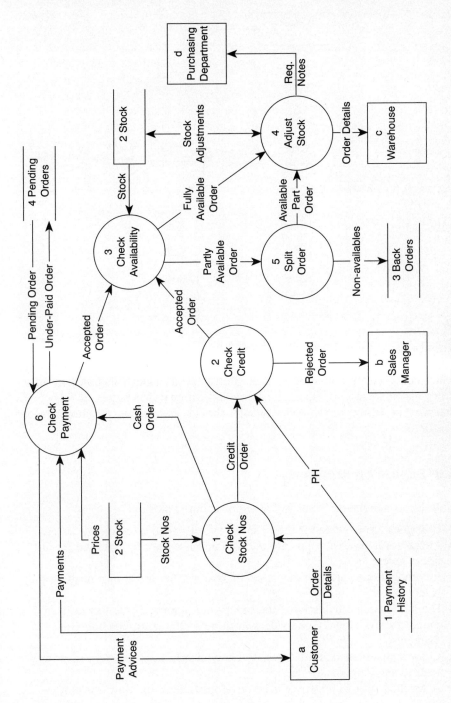

Figure 4.13

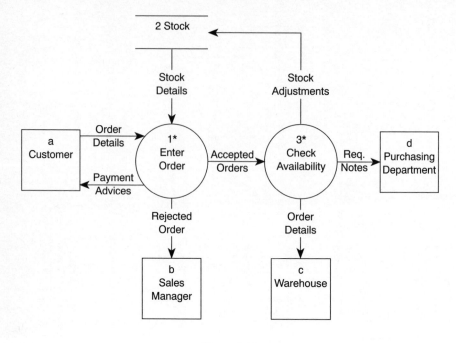

Figure 4.14

which are used by this system. It is allowable on context diagrams to have flows that involve only external entities and external data stores. If a context diagram is being used, no externals should appear on the lower-level diagrams.

4.6 Explosion summary

Now let us summarize what we've learnt about explosion:

- Processes are exploded if they can be usefully split into sub-processes.
- Local stores on explosions are allowed and need not be reflected on the upper levels.
- External entities are not shown on explosions, but are shown at the top level.
- Diagram sets are balanced if the inputs and outputs of the parent processes are logically equivalent to those of the corresponding child diagrams.
- Context diagrams could be used to show clearly how a system interfaces with its environment.
- A levelled set of DFDs might be developed either top-down or bottom-up.

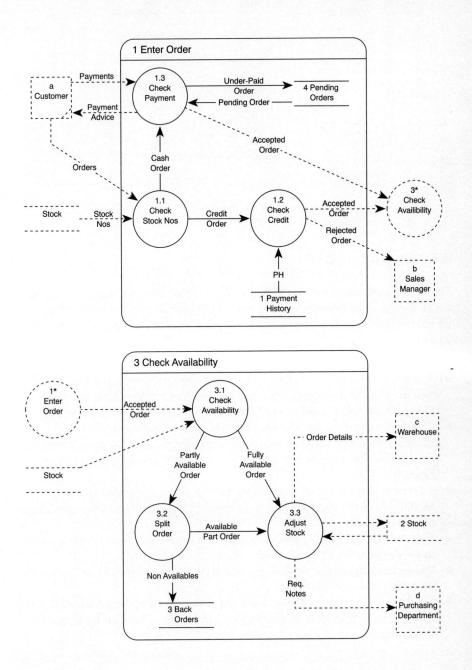

Figure 4.15

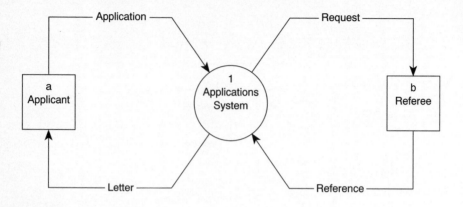

Figure 4.16

4.7 Benefits of DFDs

That concludes our look at DFDs. In this and in the previous two chapters we've seen how to draw current logical DFDs, how to develop required logical DFDs and how to develop exploded DFDs. We've also looked at different DFD styles.

The use of DFDs has a number of benefits:

- A structured technique helps the analyst to organize the details of the system being investigated. This not only prevents the analyst from disappearing under a deluge of information, it also helps understanding.
- A precise picture of the system is given. This avoids costly misunderstandings between users and developers (or between different developers). Incomplete knowledge is soon highlighted by gaps in the diagram.
- A concise description of the system can be given compared to the earlier 'techniques' of system flowcharting and English narrative. This also helps communication.
- System boundaries are clearly shown at an early stage so that there can be no misunderstanding about the scope of the system.
- The model is useful to both users and developers, so there's no notion of producing two specifications.
- Finally, because the diagrams are clear and easy to understand, users are encouraged to take part in the project and become enthusiastic about the development.

At this point, we have an extremely useful model, but it's still only a sketch of a system. In the next chapter we'll see how to flesh out this skeleton by developing a data dictionary.

CHAPTER 5

Recording data in the data dictionary

5.1 Introduction

In the previous three chapters we saw how to build up a useful model of a system using data flow diagrams. The technique of explosion within these diagrams is a powerful way of breaking a complex problem down into a number of simpler ones. However, we still haven't reached the level of detail that would be needed by a developer to actually build the system. To do this we need to record more information about data and about processes. This is done in a data dictionary. In this chapter we'll be looking at how to record data in the data dictionary, and in the next chapter at how to record processes. We'll be concentrating primarily on a Gane and Sarson-style data dictionary, but we will look at other styles at the end of this chapter.

5.2 Data dictionaries

The term data dictionary is popular, but is often used in computing to describe two different things. Some people think of a data dictionary as a collection of details about data within a company's computer systems. What we mean by a data dictionary is a collection of further details about everything on a set of DFDs. The term data dictionary is a poor description of this, because we want to record details not only about data, but also about processes. A much better term would be project directory, but this isn't in common usage.

The data parts of DFDs are data flows and data stores. On the DFD we have just a name for flows and stores, but obviously we need to record the content and structure of these before we can develop software. Because we're still working with a logical model, we want a way of describing data that will accommodate any physical implementation. This is done by using a simple two-tier model comprising data elements and data structures. Data elements are items of data that we don't want to split down any further, like an invoice number or a product description. Data structures are collections of data elements and other data structures. For example, we might have a data structure of Customer Details as follows:

```
Customer-Details
        Customer-No
        Customer-Name
        Customer-Address
                Street
                Area
                Town
                County
```

This is made up of two data elements: customer number and customer name, and a data structure, customer address. The data structure customer address is itself made up of a number of data elements: street, area, town, county.

So, what do we want to record in the data dictionary about data elements and data structures? Well, for every entry in the data dictionary we want to record a name and a short description. Also, there might be 'aliases' of the name that we want to record. For example, some departments in a company might refer to a 'delivery address', while others call it a 'despatch address'. Also, these might be coded in the company's computer systems in different ways. If all these are really the same thing, we want to record the detail in the data dictionary only once. However, we do want to capture all the alternative names, or aliases.

For data elements, it's important to record values. To do this it's helpful to view each element as either discrete or continuous. Discrete data elements take on only certain predefined values. For example, a job might have codes and meanings recorded in the data dictionary, as follows:

```
01  –  Systems Analyst
02  –  Programmer
03  –  Data Base Administrator
```

Continuous data elements may take on any value over a given range. For example, a salary or a delivery time might have the limits of the range recorded in the data dictionary as

```
Salary        –  10,000 – 40,000
Delivery Time  –  9.00 – 17.00
```

We might also specify cross-check information, for example that job code 02, programmer, should have a salary in the bottom half of the recorded salary range. The main reason for recording this information for data elements is for validation. In Chapter 3 we saw how DFDs might change when considering data input by the provision of new processes and new links to data stores. If we are to perform a validation check in this way we must have something to check the incoming data against. This will be provided by the codes and ranges recorded for the data elements.

The last thing that we want to record for data elements is their length. At an early stage, this might be just in terms of the number of digits or characters, later of the internal representation in the computer. This is obviously directly useful at the implementation stage in programs and database descriptions. It might also be used earlier for sizing, that is, for calculating the size of records, and therefore files or databases, and making decisions about the hardware and software necessary for the system.

For data structures, the main thing that we want to record is the structure of the data. As we saw earlier, this may be made up of data elements and data structures.

It's well accepted in computing that most programs are composed of just three basic constructs – sequence, selection and iteration. A sequence is where one statement follows on directly from another on a single path through the program, a selection where there's a choice of paths through the program, and an iteration where there's a looping structure in the program. These constructs can also be applied to data, and are used to bind the data elements and data structures into the data structure that we're describing in the data dictionary. The notation for sequence, selection and iteration in a data structure is as follows.

For a sequence, the names of the data elements and data structures are just listed down the page in order. The following is a data structure, address, that is made up of four data elements: a street, followed by an area, followed by a town, followed by a county. The order in which these are put down does make a difference: it implies sequence. Notice how the contents of the data structure are indented from its name.

```
ADDRESS
        STREET
        AREA
        TOWN
        COUNTY
```

For a selection, two or more names are written in braces, as below. This means that the data structure, payment, contains either a cheque number or a credit card number following the customer number, but not both.

```
┌─────────────────────────────────────────────┐
│  PAYMENT                                      │
│        CUSTOMER-NO.                           │
│                                               │
│         ⎧  CHEQUE-NO    ⎫                      │
│         ⎨ ─────────────  ⎬                     │
│         ⎩ CREDIT-CARD-NO ⎭                     │
│                                               │
└─────────────────────────────────────────────┘
```

For an iteration, the name is followed by an asterisk and a range in brackets, as for the invoice items below. The asterisk merely denotes that there is an iteration, while the range identifies how many times the item might repeat. So this means that each invoice contains a number of invoice items, and that there is always at least one and never more than twenty.

```
┌─────────────────────────────────────────────┐
│  INVOICE                                      │
│        CUSTOMER-NO                            │
│        CUSTOMER-ADDRESS                       │
│        INVOICE-ITEMS * (1-20)                 │
│              STOCK-NO                         │
│              QUANTITY                         │
│              PRICE                            │
└─────────────────────────────────────────────┘
```

Notice that this time the data structure 'invoice' contains two data elements, customer number and customer address, followed by another data structure, invoice items. Notice also how the contents of invoice items (the data elements stock no, quantity and price) are also indented. What we really mean by saying that the data structure invoice items might repeat up to twenty times is that its contents might repeat up to twenty times.

The notation has been extended to identify optionality by using square brackets, as below. This means that an address will always contain a street, a town and a county and may contain an area.

```
┌─────────────────────────────────────────────┐
│  ADDRESS                                      │
│        STREET                                 │
│        [ AREA ]                               │
│        TOWN                                   │
│        COUNTY                                 │
└─────────────────────────────────────────────┘
```

That covers what needs to be recorded for data structures and data elements, but remember that they are not an end in themselves; they are only a means of describing data flows and data stores. In addition, data flows will have their source and destination recorded, and data stores will have the flows in and out recorded.

Both data flows and data stores might also have volume and current physical implementation recorded. For example, for a data flow of invoices, we might record that there are currently 200 per week on three-part pre-printed stationery. For a data store of customer details, we might record that there are 3000 records in a database package on a PC.

Before we look at an example, let's recap on the contents of the data part of the data dictionary. For each data element we'll record name, description, aliases, values, cross-check information and length. For each data structure we'll record name, description and the structure of the data. For each data flow we'll record name, description, data structure, source, destination, volume and current physical implementation. For each data store we'll record name, description, data structure, flows in, flows out, volume and current physical implementation.

As to the format of the data dictionary, the simplest way to think about it is as an alphabetical card index. There will be one card for each data flow and each data store on the set of DFDs. These will record the information listed above, including information about data elements and data structures, which in turn will have their own entries. There might be further entries for aliases, but the detail will be recorded only once.

When using a CASE tool, the DFD and data dictionary are often much more integrated. This means that the data dictionary is much more distributed, with the textual detail in the data dictionary underlying the graphical objects of the DFD. For example, when looking at a DFD in a CASE tool, the data dictionary entry for a particular flow might be revealed by double clicking it.

Now, let's look at an example to see how all this works in practice. In general, the building of the data part of the data dictionary is time consuming, but fairly simple, involving a lot of investigation and recording. However, it would be impossible to proceed without the detail that it provides about the data of the system. Among all this perspiration, the only inspiration that is needed concerns the description of the data structure in terms of sequence, selection and iteration, and it is this that we will be concentrating on in the examples and exercises.

EXAMPLE 5.1

We might have a data flow, Weekly Sales Report, on a DFD, as in Figure 5.1. The actual report layout is as in Table 5.1. Here we have

Figure 5.1

Table 5.1 *Weekly sales report*

Branch	Projected	Actual	Difference
3 Ashington	59,498	63,595	4,097
11 Fulwell	36,822	54,471	17,649
12 S-Shields	100,072	141,926	41,854
Area 1 total	**196,392**	**259,992**	**63,600**
1 Hartlep'l	55,365	69,098	13,733
7 Linthorpe	66,895	89,148	22,253
9 Stockton	43,627	62,010	18,383
Area 2 total	**165,887**	**220,256**	**54,369**
Co, total	**674,594**	**799,714**	**125,122**

the projected and actual sales figures for each branch, and the difference between the two figures. Notice that the branches are arranged into areas, and that on the report we have area totals and an overall company total.

The first thing to do is to try to describe the data structure for this report in terms of sequence, selection and iteration. If we leave aside the totalling for the moment, the report has a very simple structure: it's just an iteration of branch sales details. So, we could start our data structure as below. If we know that there will always be twelve branches, say, we can add the number of iterations in brackets after the asterisk.

```
WEEKLY-SALES-REPORT
     BRANCH-SALES * (3)
```

For each branch we record the branch number and name, projected sales, actual sales and difference. This is a sequence that we can add to the data structure as follows:

```
WEEKLY-SALES-REPORT
     BRANCH-SALES * (12)
          BRANCH
          PROJECTED
          ACTUAL
          DIFFERENCE
```

In general, any simple report in columns is made up of an iteration going down the page, and a sequence going across. Notice the way that indentation is used to give meaning to the data structure. In this way we can 'read' the data structure, as follows:

'The weekly sales report is made up of an iteration of branch sales details. For each branch sales, there's a branch, followed by a projected sales figure, followed by an actual sales figure, followed by a difference.'

If we now consider the totalling on the report, we can see that at the highest level we have an iteration of area sales details, followed by company totals. If we know that there are always going to be four areas, say, we could expand the structure as below. Notice that the number of iterations for branch sales has now been reduced to three. It has been assumed that there will be the same number of branches in each area, so the number of branch sales figures that we have for each area is three. Before we included the area sales structure, the iteration of branch sales referred to the number of branches on the whole report.

```
WEEKLY-SALES-REPORT
    AREA-SALES * (4)
        BRANCH-SALES * (3)
            BRANCH
            PROJECTED
            ACTUAL
            DIFFERENCE
    COMPANY TOTALS
```

We are not quite finished yet because, although we have an iteration of branch sales for each area, we still don't have area totals. These should follow the branch sales iteration within the area sales structure, as follows:

```
WEEKLY-SALES-REPORT
    AREA-SALES * (4)
        BRANCH-SALES * (3)
            BRANCH
            PROJECTED
            ACTUAL
            DIFFERENCE
        AREA-TOTALS
    COMPANY TOTALS
```

We can now read the structure again. Notice how this goes down level by level following the indentation:

'The weekly sales report is made up of an iteration of area sales details, followed by company totals. For each area sales there's an iteration of branch sales details followed by an area total. For each branch sales, there's a branch, followed by a projected sales figure, followed by an actual sales figure, followed by a difference.'

Now that we've got a data structure we need to think carefully about how to record it in the data dictionary. At the top level, the weekly sales report is the data flow from the DFD, and the whole indented structure above is its data structure. This will form the basis for the entry for the data flow, together with the other things that were talked about earlier, like the source and destination objects.

This is the only point of contact with the DFD and everything else in the structure is a data structure or data element. Any item that has a sub-structure is a data structure. So, in this example, area sales and branch sales will be described in the data dictionary as a data structure. That is, we record the name, description and indented data structure. For branch sales, we would record its indented structure as the data structure. For area sales we could record its whole indented structure as its data structure. However, the structure indented for branch sales has already been recorded, so it could be left out.

Anything at the bottom level of the structure (that is, with no sub-structure) is a data element. So, in this example we have branch, projected sales, actual sales, difference, area totals and company totals. If we have a sample, as we do in this case, we should be able to see actual values for the data elements on it. There's no problem with the first four as they all relate to individual cells on the report. However, the totals are different. They relate to whole lines on the report and are really data structures that we could break down as below. These two structures could be described similarly to the ones that we were looking at earlier.

AREA-TOTALS	COMPANY-TOTALS
DESCRIPTION	DESCRIPTION
PROJECTED	PROJECTED
ACTUAL	ACTUAL
DIFFERENCE	DIFFERENCE

Some of the information recorded for data elements is trivial, so we'll consider only how to record values, length and cross-check information for the data elements in this example. To decide on the values to record for each data element, we have to decide if it is discrete or continuous. Branch is discrete. The codes and meanings that we'd record would be the branch numbers and names. Description is also discrete. There are really no codes here, just a number of descriptions to record. Projected & Actual Sales and Difference are all continuous. Here we don't want to specify individual values, just the limits of the range. This could be arrived at by inspecting the report and talking to the people involved about likely trends. There's a difficult balance to strike here between making the validation checks sufficiently tight and allowing room for change. For example, the lowest Actual Sales figure on the report is 54,471 and the highest is 141,926. It is unlikely that we'd just specify this as a range in the data dictionary without further investigation. This might not be a typical week, sales might be significantly higher (or lower) at other times of the year (like Christmas), sales might tend to rise with inflation, and so on. We have to decide on the range so that it's useful as a validation check, but won't mean that the software needs to be constantly amended to take account of changes.

The length of a data element is straightforward. Its just the number of characters of the biggest value for discrete data elements, and the number of digits of the top of the range for continuous data elements.

So, for Description the biggest value is 'Company Total'. Therefore the length is thirteen, the number of characters in the description. For Projected Sales, we could define a range of 30,000–150,000. The length could then be recorded as 6, the number of digits in the range maximum.

Finally, we need to specify the cross-check information. The only obvious cross-check is that Difference should be the difference between Projected Sales and Actual Sales. In fact, when you realize that difference is derivable, you wonder if it's worth recording in the data dictionary at all.

Any other cross-checks would need further investigation. For example, we might expect the Actual Sales figure to be within a certain percentage of the Projected Sales figure, but we'd need to talk to the people involved to find out if this was true, and what the 'certain percentage' might be.

5.3 Data flow summary

So, we've seen how to take a sample of a data flow and derive a number of data dictionary entries. Before we move on, it's useful to summarize what we've seen.

First, a data structure is developed for the whole data flow in terms of sequence, selection and iteration. Indentation is used to identify sub-structures and should allow the structure to be 'read'. This becomes the basis for the data flow entry.

We then inspect the complete structure and identify data structures and data elements. Those items that have sub-structures are data structures and those that don't are data elements. The entry for each data structure is basically its sub-structure with any unnecessary lower-level detail removed.

Six things are recorded for each data element, but probably the most important is values. These are either a set of discrete values or the limits of a continuous range. Care needs to be taken when specifying range limits. The range should form the basis for a useful validation check, but it shouldn't be so tight that it's soon out of date. Formulation of ranges, and any cross-checks between data elements, are likely to be the subject of further investigation by the analyst.

5.4 Data stores

In the previous example, we concentrated on a data dictionary entry for a data flow, Weekly Sales Report. A data dictionary entry for a data store would be approached in exactly the same way. The only additional point to bear in mind is that data stores almost always involve an iteration at the very top level. Following on from the previous example, if there was a store that held the Weekly Sales Reports for the last year, the data dictionary entry would be

```
WEEKLY-SALES-REPORT * (52)
        AREA-SALES * (4)
                BRANCH-SALES * (3)
                        BRANCH
                        PROJECTED
                        ACTUAL
                        DIFFERENCE
                AREA-TOTALS
        COMPANY TOTALS
```

The only difference from the earlier data dictionary entry for the data flow is the '*' and '(52)' after the main structure name, Weekly Sales Report. All this means is that we're storing details of 52 Weekly Sales Reports in this data store. However, this information will be captured when we record the volume of the store so it could be omitted. In this case, the data structure for the Weekly Sales Report data store would be the same as for the Weekly Sales Report data flow.

Exercise 5.1

Develop a data structure for the report sample below and define the contained data structures and data elements.

	Delivery times		
BR.no.	Mon	Tue	Wed
1	0720 Fresh	0720 Fresh	0715 Fresh
	1307 Groc SO	1835 Bulk Ev	1235 Prom
2	0720 Fresh	0700 Fresh	0705 Fresh
	0750 Groc SO	1315 Groc	1420 Bulk
3	0720 Fresh	0710 Fresh	0715 Fresh
	1100 Groc SO	0515 Groc NT	1345 Groc
	1400 Groc	0515 Bulk NT	1415 Bulk

Fresh = Fresh Food   SO = Standing Order
Groc = Grocery   NT = Night Time
Bulk = Bulk Delivery   Ev = Evening
Prom = Promotion

The sample above just gives detail from the top left-hand corner of a typical report. Assume that there are always 13 branches on the report. Also assume that each branch always gets at least one delivery Monday to Saturday, and never more than five, and that there are no deliveries on Sundays.

A solution to this exercise is walked through in the Appendix, starting on p. 199.

5.5 Data dictionary styles

Before we leave the subject of recording data in the data dictionary, it's useful to highlight differences in data dictionary styles. We've been looking at the Gane and Sarson notation and contents in this chapter, but there are really no fundamental differences from Yourdon. The notation for sequence, selection and iteration is different, so the first data structure below in Gane and Sarson notation looks quite different from the second in Yourdon notation. Apart from that, the Yourdon data dictionary is not quite as detailed, so items like length and cross-check information are not recorded for data elements, and volume and current physical implementation are not recorded for data flows and data stores.

```
ORDER
       CUSTOMER ID
       CUSTOMER NAME
       [ADDRESS]
       DETAILS * (10)
```

> ORDER = CUSTOMER ID + CUSTOMER NAME +
> (ADDRESS) + {DETAILS} 10

In SSADM, there is a data dictionary that underlies the DFD similarly to the Yourdon method, but there are some differences in format. Data stores are not modelled in the data dictionary as such, but form an input to entity relationship diagramming, which we will be looking at in Chapter 7. Data flows are modelled in the data dictionary in a two-tier fashion. At the top level there is a forms-based I/O Description which records the source, destination and name of the flow, plus its contents. The contents are unstructured on the I/O Description and may be thought of as a list of data elements. The structure is provided by using Jackson's well-known graphical notation for sequence, selection and iteration to model the contents. These are called I/O structures in SSADM.

5.6 Summary

In this chapter we've looked at how to record data in the data dictionary. We've seen how to describe data in terms of data elements and data structures, and how this is tied back into data flows and data stores. We've also seen how to identify data structures and data elements from samples and how to define a structure in terms of sequence, selection and iteration. Finally, we've looked at different data dictionary styles.

Remember, though, that the data dictionary should record information about all things on a DFD, not just the data parts. Therefore, in the next chapter we'll look at how to record processes in the data dictionary.

CHAPTER 6

Recording processes in the data dictionary

6.1 Introduction

In the previous chapter we saw how to record data in the data dictionary. In this chapter we're going to look at how to record processes.

The connection between the DFD and the data dictionary is simple for processes. We want to record a process specification (or 'minispec' as Yourdon calls them) for each process on the DFD that isn't exploded. We'll look at the problems with using English narrative for process specification, and the alternatives offered by structured methods. The two alternatives that we'll look at in detail are Structured English and decision tables.

6.2 English narrative

Why not use English for process specification? Well, for a start, there are so many ways of saying the same thing. This can lead to process specifications that are verbose and unclear. Consider these two statements:

Multiply x by y unless y is negative, in which case multiply x by the modulus of y.

If the value of y is less than zero, multiply y by -1 and calculate the product as being x times the new value of y. If the value of y is positive, calculate the product as being just x times y with no adjustment to y before doing the sum.

Are these two statements the same? Well, it's difficult to say immediately, but if you think about it for a little while you'll see that they are. It would be so much better if there was a standard way of saying things. Also, notice how long the second statement takes to say exactly the same as the first; and how this obscures the meaning. We want something that is more concise and clear.

Another problem with English is ambiguity. This is disastrous in a specification because the writer doesn't realize that the specification is ambiguous, and the reader could take entirely the wrong meaning. A common problem area is when there is an *and* and *or* in the same sentence.

Consider another statement:

'Orders for less than 20 items and for local delivery or for less than £50 get shipped the same day.'

Do orders for less than £50 get shipped the same day? Well, it depends how you read the sentence. If you read it with the emphasis on the *or* it appears that they do. However, if you read it with the emphasis on the *and*, it's not clear. In mathematics and programming languages, *and* and *or* are governed by formal rules of precedence, but this is not so in English and can lead to ambiguity. The meaning of the sentence above is for the reader to interpret. Obviously, we want to get round this problem and find a way of specifying processes that is not ambiguous.

Also, it's easy to be vague and gloss over things that we're not quite sure of in English. For example, what is meant by a local delivery in the previous statement? ... within 10 miles? ... within 50 miles? We want our process specification to be as precise as possible.

6.3 Structured English

So, if we're not going to use English as a process specification tool, what alternatives have we got? The main alternative recommended by structured methods is Structured English. This is a form of English with a limited number of constructs and a limited vocabulary.

We saw in the previous chapter that most programs are made up of just three structures – sequence, selection and iteration. Given that ultimately we want to convert the specifications to software in some way, these are really the only constructs that we need.

We can limit the vocabulary within the process specifications. We will use

- Imperative verbs, like multiply or print
- Data dictionary terms, either names or sub-ranges
- 'Construct' words
- A little English for readability
- Mathematical symbols, and
- Labels.

More about these in the examples below. There are usually conventions for identifying data dictionary terms and construct words. We'll underline data dictionary terms and write construct words in capitals. Let's now look at each of the three constructs in turn.

The sequence is a series of imperative statements as follows. Notice the underlining of data dictionary terms.

```
    ---   ---   ---   ---
    DO Calculate-Invoice-Total
    ---   ---   ---   ---
Caluclate-Invoice-Total
    Get price given item-no
    Multiply quantity by price giving gross
    DO Calculate-Discount
    Invoice-Total = gross - discount
```

To help understanding, process specifications are often written in a hierarchical, top-down fashion, similar to the way that sets of DFDs are developed by explosion. To allow this, DO is used to carry out a block of statements at a lower level. For example, above we have the statement 'DO Calculate-Invoice-Total'. Further down the process specification, under the label 'Calculate-Invoice-Total', we can see exactly what is meant by this. Like DFDs, this decomposition could go on indefinitely. In 'Calculate-Invoice-Total' we can see the statement 'DO Calculate-Discount'. Lower down in the process specification we would expect to find another label 'Calculate-Discount' containing a number of statements defining exactly what we mean by that, and so on.

The second construct is selection. This shows alternatives in the process specification. The construct words IF, THEN, ELSE, SO and ENDIF are used, as in

```
IF delivery is local
        THEN Add £5 to Invoice-Total
ELSE (delivery not local)
        SO Add £20 to Invoice-Total
ENDIF
```

There are several points here. Notice how indentation is used to help the meaning and how the reverse of the original condition is stated for the ELSE part. Some people think that this is long-winded, though, and may miss it out, together with some of the construct words. Really, if indentation is being used, THEN and SO serve little purpose. Also, remember that the ELSE part is optional. Notice that 'local' is underlined to denote that it is a data dictionary term. We criticized English earlier for using vague terms like 'local', but here it would be defined elsewhere in the data dictionary exactly what we mean by the term.

If the selection is more complex, we can nest IF constructs as in the following. Notice how one is nested inside the other and how the indentation is preserved. We could nest sequences within selections similarly. That is, the action for a condition could be more complex than a single statement.

```
IF delivery is local
        IF Order-value > £50
                Add £1 to Invoice-Total
        ELSE
                Add £5 to Invoice-Total
        ENDIF
ELSE
        Add £20 to Invoice-Total
ENDIF
```

If the selection becomes too complex, it may be better to use a different process specification tool as we'll see later. If there are more than two alternatives, we can use a sequence of IF constructs as in the following. Alternatively, we could use a CASE statement similar to the one used in some programming languages.

```
IF x = 1
        Add B to A
ENDIF
IF x = 2
        Add C To A
ENDIF
IF x = 3
        . . .
```

The last construct is iteration. This details loops or repetitions in the process specification. The construct words REPEAT and UNTIL may be used as in the following:

```
REPEAT
        DO Calculate-Invoice-Total
        Print Invoice
UNTIL no more Sales-Details
```

Here, a sequence of statements is repeated until a stop condition becomes true. Notice how the indentation makes it clear exactly what is to be repeated.

Some people prefer to use DOWHILE . . . ENDDO instead of REPEAT . . . UNTIL. This would change our last example as follows.

```
DOWHILE more Sales-Details
        DO Calculate-Invoice-Total
        Print Invoice
ENDDO
```

Notice that the condition is now reversed and stated at the top of the loop.

REPEAT constructs can be nested inside each other in the same way as IF constructs. In fact, any of the constructs can be nested within any of the other constructs.

So, how does Structured English get round the problems that we anticipated with ordinary English? Well, we do now have a standard way of saying things, which should cut out much of the verbosity and make the meaning clearer. Also, vagueness should be avoided because we're using terms defined in the data dictionary.

Finally, ambiguity now has much less opportunity to arise. In fact, it is only in the conditions for selections and iterations that it might occur. Even then, it is often possible to write the specification using nesting to avoid the use of composite conditions using *and* and *or*. If it can't be avoided, we use the rule common in programming languages that *and*s have more weight in conditions than *or*s.

EXAMPLE 6.1

Now that we've seen the conventions of Structured English, let's look at an example to see how the constructs and vocabulary fit together. The Weekly Sales Report that we saw in the previous chapter might appear on a DFD as in Figure 6.1, and we developed a data structure for this.

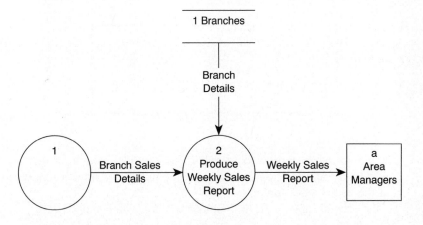

Figure 6.1

```
WEEKLY-SALES REPORT
      AREA-SALES * (4)
            BRANCH-SALES * (3)
                  BRANCH
                  PROJECTED
                  ACTUAL
                  DIFFERENCE
            AREA-TOTALS
      COMPANY TOTALS
```

Reading the data structure, the report is an iteration of area sales followed by company totals. Each area sales is an iteration of branch sales followed by area totals. And each branch sales is a sequence of branch, followed by projected, followed by actual, followed by difference. This data structure refers to the data flow Weekly Sales Report on the DFD in Figure 6.1. If we are to develop a process specification for the process Produce Weekly Sales Report on that diagram, we must model the inputs as well as the output of the process.

The first input is a flow of Branch Sales Details from a previous process. This could contain actual sales figures for each branch. To make life easier, we will assume that the branch sales details are presented in the right order to produce the report. That is, the details are sorted in ascending order on branch number within area number. Therefore, the data structure for this flow could be

```
Branch-Sales-Details
      Weekly Sales * (12)
            Area-No
            Branch-No
            Actual
```

There's an iteration of Weekly Sales, one for each branch on the report, and each iteration contains an area number, a branch number and the actual sales figure.

The second input is from a Branches store which supplies the background data necessary to produce the report. The data structure for the flow could be

```
Branch-Details
        Branch-No
        Branch-Name
        Projected
```

Here we have a structure that contains a simple sequence of Branch Number, Branch Name and Projected Sales. We will assume that there is a structure in the store like this for each branch.

To produce the Structured English for the process, we need to look at the report that we want to produce. The first two areas and the company totals are shown in Table 6.1. Basically, we have some headings at the top, some company totals at the bottom, and in the middle we're repeatedly writing out branch sales (and, intermittently, area totals).

Table 6.1 *Weekly sales report*

Branch	Projected	Actual	Difference
3 Ashington	59,498	63,595	4,097
11 Fulwell	36,822	54,471	17,649
12 S-Shields	100,072	141,926	41,854
Area 1 total	**196,392**	**259,992**	**63,600**
1 Hartlep'l	55,365	69,098	13,733
7 Linthorpe	66,895	89,148	22,253
9 Stockton	43,627	62,010	18,383
Area 2 total	**165,887**	**220,256**	**54,369**
Co. total	**674,594**	**799,714**	**125,122**

So, we could start our Structured English as follows:

```
Produce Weekly Sales Report
        Write Headings
        DOWHILE
        ENDDO
        Write Company-Totals
```

Notice the use of imperative verbs, the underlining of data dictionary terms, and the way that construct words are written in capitals. It stands out that Headings isn't underlined, and therefore isn't in the data dictionary. On reflection, it probably is not necessary for it to be, but it was good that the specification drew our attention to it.

At this point we haven't said anything about the loop in the middle, except that there will be one, so we need to think about that next. The thing that's driving the process is the Branch Sales Details flow. It provides

the actual sales figures, as well as the branch number that will allow the
Branches store to be accessed to pick up the branch names and the
projected sales figures. So, all the time that there are more iterations of
Weekly Sales, we want to continue. Therefore, we can add a condition to
the DOWHILE:

```
Produce Weekly Sales Report
    Write Headings
    DOWHILE more Weekly-Sales
    ENDDO
    Write Company-Totals
```

So, what do we do when we get some weekly sales? Well, we always
write a branch sales line on the report. Also, if the branch is in a new area,
we'll write out an area totals line first for the previous area. This could be
added to our Structured English as follows. Notice the use of the DO
construct word to identify something that we'll specify in more detail later.

```
Produce Weekly Sales Report
    Write Headings
    DOWHILE more Weekly-Sales
        IF different Area-No
            Write Area-Totals
        ENDIF
        DO Output-Branch-Sales
    ENDDO
    Write Company-Totals
```

It's important to realize that we're not at the program level here. It's not
necessary at this stage to go on to define exactly what we mean by Write
Area-Totals or Write Company-Totals because this is a simple piece of
coding. Also, there are no explicit file reads here, although this is implied
in the statement 'DOWHILE more Weekly-Sales'. Further, we don't say
how to recognize the end of weekly sales. This is because it will depend on
the eventual software implementation, and we are still working at the
logical level. The software implementation might not even be chosen at this
stage. In other places, we're not precise about how things are to be done,
we just say what is to be done. For example, recognizing a different area
might require us to store the previous area number and compare it to the
present one. Also, we'd have to have some way of dealing with this the
first time through the loop. However, we don't get into this level of coding
detail while we're writing process specifications.

We do try to get things logically correct, though, and as it stands at the moment we have no way of producing the last set of area totals. When we find that there are no more weekly sales, we'll drop out of the loop and write company totals. On the previous pass, we'll have written the last branch sales line, but we won't have written the following area totals. Therefore, we need to add a line to the Structured English. Then when we drop out of the loop, we'll write the final area totals, followed by the company totals.

```
Produce Weekly Sales Report
        Write Headings
        DOWHILE more Weekly-Sales
                IF different Area-No
                        Write Area-Totals
                ENDIF
                DO Output-Branch-Sales
        ENDDO
        Write Area-Totals
        Write Company-Totals
```

All that's left to do now is to specify how to write branch sales. Well, we've already got the actual sales from the Weekly Sales. Using the branch number from here, we can access the Branches store and get the branch name and projected sales figure. We can then calculate the difference between actual and projected sales and write the completed branch sales line:

```
Output-Branch-Sales
        Get Branch-Name and Projected from Branch-Details
        Calculate Diff = Actual - Projected
        Write Branch-Sales
```

We must also remember to add the figures into running area and company totals. This can just be specified without going into great detail:

```
Accumulate Area-Totals and Company-Totals
```

We can assume that Area-Totals will be cleared when we specify in more detail what we mean by 'Write Area-Totals'.

In this example we've seen how to combine sequence, selection and iteration constructs to form a process specification. We've also seen how DO is used to structure the specification, using labels. Construct words are written in capitals, data dictionary terms are underlined and imperative verbs are used, together with a little English for readability and some mathematical notation. But remember, while this looks something like a program, it is only a specification and we're not yet at the detailed coding level.

As a process specification tool, Structured English has several good features. It has standard constructs and rules, which make it clear and concise. It uses data dictionary terms, which makes it precise, and it uses nesting or rules of precedence to remove ambiguity.

Exercise 6.1

Produce Structured English for the process in the DFD in Figure 6.2.

Figure 6.2

A sample of the Delivery Times report is shown in Table 6.2 (and its data structure follows).

Table 6.2

		Delivery times	
BR.no.	Mon	Tue	Wed
1	1307 Groc SO	1835 Bulk Ev	1235 Prom
2	0750 Groc SO	1315 Groc	1420 Bulk
3	1100 Groc SO	0515 Groc NT	1345 Groc

Groc = Grocery   SO = Standing Order
Bulk = Bulk Delivery   NT = Night-Time
Prom = Promotion   Ev = Evening

(The sample in Table 6.2 just gives detail from the top left-hand corner of a typical report. Assume that there are always 13 branches on the report. Also assume that each branch always gets one delivery Monday to Saturday, and that there are no deliveries on Sundays.)

```
DELIVERY-TIMES
    BRANCH-DELIVERIES * (13)
        BRANCH-N0
        DAILY-DELIVERIES * (6)
            TIME
            PRODUCT
            [DELIVERY CODE]
```

(The Delivery Times data structure shown above is a simplified version of the one developed as a solution to Exercise 5.1 in the Appendix.)

The data structure for the flow into the process is shown below. The Standing Order flag in this data structure is set to 's' if the delivery is a Standing Order. Evening deliveries take place between 18.00 and 23.59, night-time deliveries between 00.00 and 06.00.

```
DELIVERIES * (13)
    BRANCH-NO
    DAILY-DELIVERIES * (6)
        TIME
        PRODUCT
        STANDING ORDER
```

A solution to this exercise is walked through in the Appendix, starting on p. 205.

A general point to note about process specifications is how well the structure of the specification corresponds to the structure of the data. In general, an iteration in the data translates into an iteration in the Structured English. This is the basis of the Jackson Structured Programming (or JSP) program design technique. While it is beyond the scope of this book, it is a natural sequel to structured methods of analysis and design where the data is described in terms of sequence, selection and iteration.

6.4 Process specification styles

There are few differences between Yourdon and Gane & Sarson in the area of Structured English. However, Gane and Sarson do recommend two variations.

6.4.1 Tight English

The first is Tight English, which is less formal than Structured English, and therefore less daunting for non-computer people. The aim is to offer the specifier similar benefits to Structured English, but to be a little less terse for users. We won't go into Tight English in much detail, but it's useful just to look at an example. The Tight English version of Exercise 6.1 is

---

To produce the Delivery Times Report
1. Write out the headings
2. Take each block of information about branch and process as follows:
  2.1 Print the branch no
  2.2 Take each daily delivery as follows
    2.2.1 Print Time
    2.2.2 Print Product
    2.2.3 Print delivery codes as follows
      – for deliveries with Standing Order flag = S
        print SO
      – for deliveries with Time in the range 1800–2359
        print EV
      – for deliveries with Time in the range 0000–0600
        print NT

Notice how there is more English narrative, and the constructs, capitals and underlining have all disappeared. Decimal numbering is used instead of constructs. Iterations in Tight English usually involve the word 'each', and selections the word 'for'.

6.4.2 Pseudocode

The second variation on Structured English is Pseudocode:

Open Deliveries File
    Read header record
    If filename or date incorrect, abort
    Open Report File
    Write Headings
    Blank out report line
    Read deliveries file
        at end DO Closedown
    DOWHILE more delivieries
        DO Output-Branch-Deliveries
    ENDDO

This is essentially Structured English with all the program level detail added. It's a physical version of Structured English for program design. Therefore, it shouldn't appear in the data dictionary as a process specification at this stage while we're still working on a logical model. It should merely be an evolution of the Structured English by the programmer as a preamble to coding.

Terminology is again a problem here. Many companies have process specification standards much like Structured English that they call Pseudocode. So, while these terms have precise meanings in structured methods, they might mean something different in the wider computing community.

6.5 Function definitions

SSADM is quite different from Yourdon/Gane and Sarson in the area of process specification, essentially using English narrative rather than Structured English. In fact, processes are specified using function definitions. These are forms that record various pieces of information about functions, including a function definition (process specification) in English narrative. The main difference with the sort of process specification that we have been looking at, apart from the difference in style, is that function definitions may cover more than one process from the DFD.

6.6 Decision tables

Structured English is a general-purpose process specification tool. That is, anything can be specified because it can handle sequence, selection and iteration. As we said earlier, though, if a selection becomes too complex, it may be better to use a different process specification tool. A good way of presenting complex decisions is by using a decision table. Remember, though, that decision tables can only work with Structured English. They can't stand on their own because they have no notion of sequence or iteration.

Condition Stub	Condition Entry
Action Stub	Action Entry

Figure 6.3

As you might expect for something that handles selection, a decision table is made up of conditions and actions. It has four parts: a condition stub, a condition entry, an action stub, and an action entry, as in Figure 6.3. What we mean by these terms is probably best illustrated by an example.

EXAMPLE 6.2

Consider this narrative describing how delivery charges are calculated.

> 'If the order is worth £2000 or more, the charge is 1% of order value for deliveries within a 50-mile radius, and 1.5% for those on or outside this radius. For orders below £2000, the charge is 1.5% within a 50-mile radius, and 2% for those on or outside this radius. If express delivery is required, the above rates are doubled for deliveries not within a 50-mile radius.'

Here we have a number of conditions which combine to give us a number of actions. The first thing to do is to try to identify the conditions and enter them into the condition stub of the decision table. Clues to the presence of conditions are often given by the use of the words 'if' and 'for', and these are underlined in the excerpts from the problem statement as we walk through the example below.

So, if we look at the example, the first sentence is in three parts. The first part states 'If the order is worth £2000 or more'. We have found the first condition, Order >= £2000, and this can be entered into the condition stub (see below). The second part of the sentence continues 'the charge is 1% of order value for deliveries within a 50-mile radius'. The first part of this is an action (telling us what percentage to charge), but the second part is another condition. The third part of the sentence ('and 1.5% for those on or outside this radius') is similar to the last, with an action followed by a condition. In fact, the condition here is merely the reverse of the previous condition. Notice how it is only stated once, 'Distance >= 50 miles', in the condition stub (see below). It doesn't matter which way round the condition is stated. 'Distance < 50 miles' would have been just as good, but there is no need to enter it both ways. This will be taken care of by the condition entry, as we will see shortly. Notice also that only simple conditions are entered. That is, we don't try to construct conditions here which relate to order value *and* distance. Combinations of conditions will again be taken care of by the condition entry.

To continue with the example, the next sentence gives us only conditions that we already have, or their reverse. But the last sentence says 'If express delivery is required, the above rates are doubled for deliveries not within a 50-mile radius'. This gives us our final condition, express delivery, and completes the condition stub.

| Order > = £2000 |
| Distance > = 50 miles |
| Express delivery |

In the condition entry, we want to generate a rule for every possible combination of conditions. For n conditions, there will be 2^n combinations as long as the conditions all relate to different things. In this case, there are three conditions, so there are 2^3 rules; that is, eight rules. We add the rules to the table as numbered columns. We then complete the condition entry with Ys and Ns (for Yes and No). One way to do this is to complete the first half of the first row with Ys, and the second half of the row with Ns. Then, in the second row, the number of Ys and Ns grouped together is halved and repeated, and so on, until we arrive at Table 6.3. This way of manufacturing rules without looking at the problem is important because it assures us of completeness. If we just put a rule in the table for every action that we know about, we might miss out some combinations.

The condition part of the table is now complete and we move on to look at the action part. The action stub is completed similarly to the condition stub, but this time we're looking for actions. In this example the actions all relate to percentage charges. We noticed several actions while we were looking for conditions, and the charges of 1%, 1.5% and 2% come directly from the text in the first two sentences. The last sentence tells us that these rates could be doubled in certain circumstances, so we have to add two actions to allow for this, charging 3% and 4% (see Table 6.4).

The action entry is completed by reading through the problem and matching statements to rules in the table. The first sentence starts 'If the order is worth

Table 6.3

	1	2	3	4	5	6	7	8
Order > = £2000	Y	Y	Y	Y	N	N	N	N
Distance > = 50 miles	Y	Y	N	N	Y	Y	N	N
Express delivery	Y	N	Y	N	Y	N	Y	N

Table 6.4

	1	2	3	4	5	6	7	8
Order > = £2000	Y	Y	Y	Y	N	N	N	N
Distance > = 50 miles	Y	Y	N	N	Y	Y	N	N
Express delivery	Y	N	Y	N	Y	N	Y	N
Charge 1%								
Charge 1.5%								
Charge 2%								
Charge 3%								
Charge 4%								

Table 6.5

	1	2	3	4	5	6	7	8
Order > = £2000	Y	Y	Y	Y	N	N	N	N
Distance > = 50 miles	Y	Y	N	N	Y	Y	N	N
Express delivery	Y	N	Y	N	Y	N	Y	N
Charge 1%				X				
Charge 1.5%		X						
Charge 2%								
Charge 3%								
Charge 4%								

£2000 or more, the charge is 1% of order value for deliveries within a 50-mile radius'. Comparing this to the conditions in the condition stub, the answer to the first, Order >= £2000, is Yes. The answer to the second, Distance >= 50 miles, is No. And the answer to the third, Express delivery, is No. This matches rule 4, so we can put a cross against Charge 1% in the rule 4 column, as in Table 6.5. Completing the first sentence, we find another action, Charge 1.5%, which has the same conditions as the first, but with the distance condition reversed. This matches rule 2 in the table, so we can place our second cross as in the table.

The next sentence gives us rules 8 and 6 in the table in a similar way, giving a partially completed table as in Table 6.6

This completes the picture for deliveries where express delivery is not required. But 'If express delivery is required, the above rates are doubled for deliveries not within a 50-mile radius'. This means that any of the rules with a Y against express delivery and a Y against Distance >= 50 miles has an action of double the rate for normal deliveries. This applies to rules 1 and 5. For rule 1, we can see from rule 2 that the normal charge is 1.5%, so the express charge is 3%. Similarly for rule 5. For the last two rules, 3 and 7, the charge is the same for express as for normal deliveries. This gives us a completed table as in Table 6.7.

To simplify the finished table, it may be consolidated. That is, if two rules differ by one condition, and have the same action, they may be combined. In

Table 6.6

	1	2	3	4	5	6	7	8
Order > = £2000	Y	Y	Y	Y	N	N	N	N
Distance > = 50 miles	Y	Y	N	N	Y	Y	N	N
Express delivery	Y	N	Y	N	Y	N	Y	N
Charge 1%				X				
Charge 1.5%		X						X
Charge 2%						X		
Charge 3%								
Charge 4%								

Table 6.7

	1	2	3	4	5	6	7	8
Order > = £2000	Y	Y	Y	Y	N	N	N	N
Distance > =50 miles	Y	Y	N	N	Y	Y	N	N
Express delivery	Y	N	Y	N	Y	N	Y	N
Charge 1%			X	X				
Charge 1.5%		X					X	X
Charge 2%						X		
Charge 3%	X							
Charge 4%					X			

our table, this is true for rules 3 and 4. They have the same action, and differ by only one condition, express delivery. Therefore, we could combine them as in Table 6.8. We could combine rules 7 and 8 in the same way. The dash in the condition entry indicates indifference to the condition. Note that we could not combine conditions 1 and 2, or conditions 5 and 6. While both of these pairs differ by only one condition, they have different actions.

Table 6.8 is an example of a limited entry table. That is, the entry parts are limited to Y, N or – for conditions; and X or space for actions. We can develop what's known as an extended entry table. That is, all the entries in the table are extended to be more meaningful.

So, we could have extended entries for the actions as in Table 6.9. Notice how this makes the table much smaller and easier to understand.

Similarly, we could extend the condition entry. For example, we could code type of delivery as E (for express) or N (for normal). This would change the

Table 6.8

	1	2	3/4	5	6	7/8
Order > = £2000	Y	Y	Y	N	N	N
Distance > =50 miles	Y	Y	N	Y	Y	N
Express delivery	Y	N	–	Y	N	–
Charge 1%			X			
Charge 1.5%		X				X
Charge 2%					X	
Charge 3%	X					
Charge 4%				X		

Table 6.9

	1	2	3/4	5	6	7/8
Order > = £2000	Y	Y	Y	N	N	N
Distance > =50 miles	Y	Y	N	Y	Y	N
Express delivery	Y	N	–	Y	N	–
Charge	3	1.5	1	4	2	1.5

Table 6.10

	1	2	3/4	5	6	7/8
Order > = £2000	Y	Y	Y	N	N	N
Distance > = 50 miles	Y	Y	N	Y	Y	N
Delivery	E	N	–	E	N	–
Charge	3	1.5	1	4	2	1.5

table as in Table 6.10. This adds little to the meaning, and condition entries are usually left as limited. As it stands now Table 6.10 is a mixed entry table. That is, some of the entries are limited and some are extended.

If the decision table is not too complex, it may be presented graphically as a decision tree to help our understanding of the logic. Decision trees are usually drawn from unconsolidated, limited entry tables. For example, a decision tree of Table 6.7 is presented in Figure 6.4.

It's useful to summarize the steps that we went through in the example.

1. Extract the conditions from the problem and enter them in the condition stub.

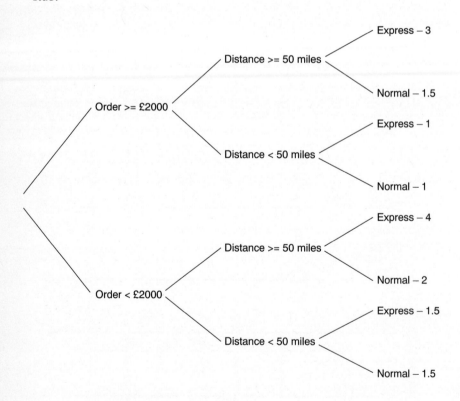

Figure 6.4

2. Calculate the number of rules and draw a numbered column in the entry part of the table for each rule.
3. Complete the condition entry with Ys and Ns.
4. Extract the actions from the problem and enter them in to the action stub.
5. Match the problem to rules in the table and complete the action entry.
6. Consolidate the table.
7. Extend the entries in the table.
8. Draw a decision tree of the table.

Exercise 6.2

Develop a decision table and a decision tree for the problem statement below.

If the age of the main driver is 25 years or more, the car is manufactured in the UK and the accident record is good, the premium charged is 6% of the declared value and the policy issued is a comprehensive one. If the accident record is not good, the policyholder pays the first £50 of any damage sustained, the premium is raised to 7% and a comprehensive policy is issued.

If the age of the main driver is 25 years or more, the car is not manufactured in the UK and the accident record is good, the policyholder pays the first £50 of any damage sustained, the premium charged is 6% of the declared value and a comprehensive policy is issued. On the other hand, if all the above conditions apply except that the accident record is not good, the premium is raised to 7% and a third-party policy only is issued.

If the age of the main driver is less than 25 years, the car is manufactured in the UK and the accident record is good, the premium charged is 6% of the declared value and the policy issued is a comprehensive one. If the accident record is not good and all other conditions apply, the premium is raised to 7% and a third-party policy only is issued.

If the age of the main driver is less than 25 years, the car is not manufactured in the UK and the accident record is good, the policyholder pays the first £50 of any damage sustained, the premium charged is 8% of the declared value and a comprehensive policy is issued. If the accident record is not good and all other conditions apply, the clerk is instructed to decline the risk altogether and inform the applicant accordingly.

A solution to this exercise is walked through in the Appendix, starting on p. 208.

6.7 Summary

This concludes our look at recording process in the data dictionary. Remember, the link between the DFD and the process part of the data dictionary is very simple. There is a process specification (or minispec) in the data dictionary for each process that isn't exploded on the DFD. There are several ways of writing process specifications. There are a number of potential problems with English narrative, although SSADM does use this within function definitions. Generally a form of Structured English is used where there are a limited number of constructs, based on programming languages, and a limited vocabulary. This is sometimes toned down into a less terse form called Tight English. Alternatively, Pseudocode might be used for some users, or for programmers progressing the process specification through program design to coding. Decision tables and trees might be used to help in specifying complex decisions.

So, where do we take our logical model now? Well, we have a useful graphical model in the set of DFDs, and we have the underlying detail specified in the data dictionary. Therefore, we have the level of detail necessary actually to build the system and we could go on to evolve the physical model. However, some people would argue that although there are data and process in our model, it is process-orientated. That is, the fundamental objects in the model are processes and the data is merely there to allow the processes to work. Therefore, a data-orientated view is necessary to balance the model. This is provided by the entity relationship diagram, which we'll be looking at in the next chapter.

CHAPTER 7

Data modelling

7.1 Introduction

In this chapter we're going to concentrate on the data side of our model. We'll look at how to model blocks of data (or entities) and the relationships between them using entity relationship diagrams (or ERDs). This might be characterized as a 'top-down' approach to data modelling. That is, working from our knowledge of the system, we first identify blocks of data and their relationships before going on to consider the data elements, or attributes, that make up each entity. We'll also be looking at normalization. This might be characterized as a 'bottom-up' approach to data modelling. That is, we start from a complete list of attributes and split the data into smaller, simpler groupings (entities) using normalization. While these approaches appear to be contradictory, and some methods do use either one or the other, they can be complementary.

So far in this book, we've looked at how to draw DFDs to model an information system, and how to capture the fine detail relating to data and process in the data dictionary. Some would argue that this is all we need to define a logical model of a system. Others would say that data modelling techniques, like those that we're about to explore in this chapter, are the only ones necessary to define a logical model of a system. Most methods have now come to the conclusion that both sets of techniques are needed to define a complete logical model.

7.2 Entity relationship diagrams

Many structured methods now have a separate graphical data-orientated view of the system to balance the graphical process-orientated perspective given by the DFD. This is usually provided by the ERD.

Yourdon's definition of an ERD is 'a network model that describes the stored data layout of a system at a high level of abstraction'. Obviously there's some overlap with DFDs, which show data stores, but the ERD also shows the relationships between these stores. There are often teams dedicated to data and database administration, particularly in large organizations, and ERDs help the developer to communicate with these groups. In fact, the ERD is usually the logical model of the data on which the eventual physical implementation of the database is founded. It's now well accepted in computing that data is more stable than process over time, so it makes sense to build any development on a sound data model. Even for committed process modellers, the ERD gives a different perspective on the DFD and often throws up inconsistencies and omissions.

It's important to realize that ERDs are drawn early in the development life cycle. They will often be developed in parallel with the DFD, particularly if the investigation is being carried out by one person, or a small team. If the system is data-strong (that is, there's a lot of data to model and not much process), the ERD may well be developed first. Conversely, for function-strong systems, the ERD may be developed after the DFD.

So, we've considered why to develop ERDs, and when to develop them, but what is one? Well, it's not that easy to answer that question! When we looked at DFDs, although there were different notations, they had essentially the same meaning. There are, broadly speaking, two different notations for ERDs, but there are many variations and advanced features to both notations, and they may be combined. We'll look at these one at a time and see how the same example could be drawn in each notation.

7.3 Diamond notation

The first style of ERD that we'll look at is the 'diamond' notation proposed by Chen and adopted (in part) by Yourdon. In this notation, entities are drawn and named as in Figure 7.1.

It's usual to use the singular for the name. Entities are objects within the system about which we want to store data. It should be possible to identify a number of data elements for each entity. For example, the Customer entity might be made up of Customer Number, Name, Address, and so on. The data elements associated with each entity are called its attributes. It's important to realize that the Customer entity here is a type or class of data and not a particular customer. A particular customer would be called an occurrence of the Customer entity.

Sometimes, entities might be composed of sub-entities that have extra attributes associated. For example, an entity Employee may have sub-entities of Manual and Clerical. This would be drawn as in Figure 7.2.

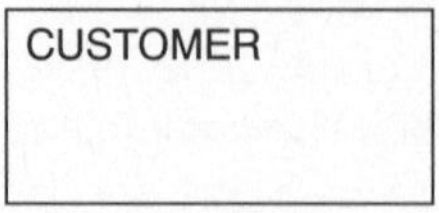

CUSTOMER

Figure 7.1

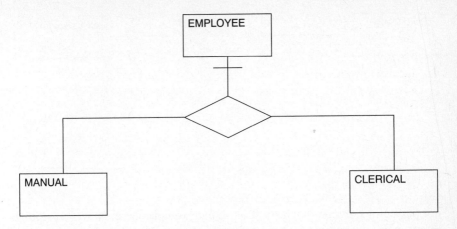

Figure 7.2

Here, we say that we have a super-type Employee, made up of two sub-types, Manual and Clerical. Employee may record Employee Number, Name, National Insurance Number, and so on; while Manual records Normal Hours, Normal Rate, Overtime Hours and Overtime Rate; and Clerical records Salary, Expenses and Pension Deductions. Generally, sub-types are only identified if there is a lot of different data to be stored for each and we will not consider them further in our examples.

Relationships are named connections between entities and are drawn as in Figure 7.3. Here we have two entities, Customer and Product, and the relationship between the two, Purchases. Relationships can be read, in this case 'Customer purchases Product'. Entities have permanent data associated with them. Relationships have no data associated with them and are like events or transactions in the life of the system. If it's necessary to record data about relationships, this is done via the rather grandly named associative object type indicators. All that this means is that if we want to record some data about purchases on this ERD, we merely redraw it as in Figure 7.4. Notice that the relationship name has disappeared from the diamond, a new entity 'Order' has been created to record the data associated with the relationship and this is connected to the diamond with an arrowed line. Relationships usually connect just two entities, but they may be used to connect more if necessary. Relationships may be seen as mandatory or optional (or obligatory and non-obligatory), and this may be shown graphically in a variety of ways, but we will

Figure 7.3

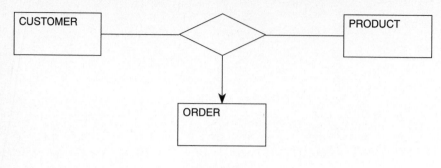

Figure 7.4

not pursue this level of sophistication in the examples here. Now, let's look at an example and see how we could construct an ERD using this notation.

EXAMPLE 7.1

Customers place orders with a mail order company for items in the catalogue. If the items are in stock, they are sent to the customer with a delivery note (a copy of which is filed). If the items are not in stock, the orders are placed in a back orders file until they can be supplied. If a customer returns any items, they are added back into stock and the copy of the delivery note is altered accordingly.

As with DFDs, there are several different ways of approaching the construction of an ERD. Some people just build up the diagram as they go, others try to spot the entities and then think about the relationships that exist between them. We'll try to build up as we go here, but we will try the other approach when we look at the other notation later. Once the problem statement is written down, nouns are often clues to potential entities, while verbs point us towards possible relationships.

The first sentence tells us 'Customers place orders with a mail order company for items in the catalogue'. If we want to store customer data in our system (for example, we might want to store name, address, telephone number, etc. for each customer) then Customer is our first entity. (In other systems, e.g. customers at a newsagents, 'Customer' might not be a valid entity because there is no data that we would want to store about it.) 'Item' is also likely to be a valid entity in this system and we could imagine storing things like item number, description and price for each item. The mail order company isn't a valid entity because it's not an object within the system, it's the place where the whole system operates. Also, the catalogue isn't a valid entity; at least, it isn't any different from what we've got already. We could store details about all the items in the catalogue, but that's already covered by the Item entity. Alternatively, we could store details like the date of publication and details of the models and the photographers used, but these aren't relevant to the system

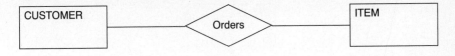

Figure 7.5

that we're looking at. So, although the catalogue is an object within our system, its not one that we want to store data about. 'Orders' is a potential entity, but we'll come back to that in a moment. We'll start with two entities, customer and item. These are both objects within the system with stored data.

The relationship between these two entities is 'orders'. This could give us a start to our diagram as in Figure 7.5. However, orders are transactions within our system that may well have data of their own, like an order number and a date. So, it might be better to make it an associative object type, as in Figure 7.6.

In the next sentence we find out 'If the items are in stock, they are sent to the customer with a delivery note (a copy of which is filed)'. Here we have a relationship between two existing entities that can be added to our diagram as in Figure 7.7. This reads right to left 'item is sent to customer'. We could show Delivery Notes as an associative object type, as in Figure 7.8. Like Orders, they represent transactions in the system that may well have data of their own, like a Delivery Note number, date, carrier etc. There is also a potential relationship here between Order and Item, as in Figure 7.9.

If we suppose that one of the data elements recorded for an Item is stock level, then Orders could be checked against Items to see if they could be despatched. In some ways, this feels more like a process on the data that we would want to capture on a DFD than a relationship between two entities on an ERD. However, we'll leave it in for now and come back to it later when we look at the second ERD notation.

'Stock' would not be another entity here because it would merely serve to duplicate the Item entity that we already have. At least, any stock information that we wanted to record could be easily added to the Item entity.

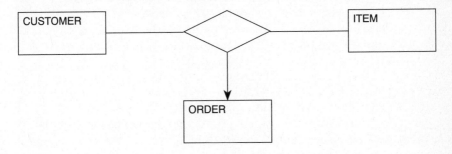

Figure 7.6

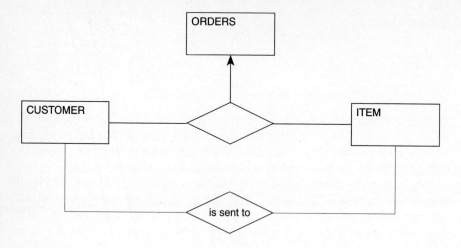

Figure 7.7

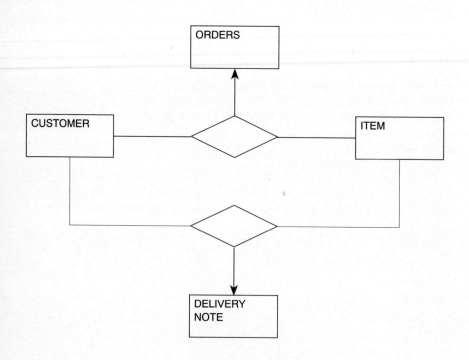

Figure 7.8

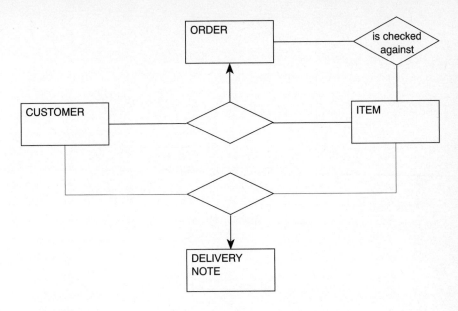

Figure 7.9

In the next sentence, we find out 'If the items are not in stock, the order is placed in a back orders file until they can be supplied'. We have already dealt with whether the items are in stock or not. Here we might identify another entity, Back Order, and add it to our diagram as in Figure 7.10.

The relationship can be read 'Order awaits supply on Back Order'. It is not clear, though, that this is necessary. We need to think carefully about what we would store for back orders. If it is similar to the information stored about Order, maybe Back Order should be a sub-type, as in Figure 7.11. If the information stored is nearly identical, say the only difference is a back order flag set to show that the order hasn't yet been supplied, maybe it should disappear from the diagram altogether. For simplicity, this is the line that we will take here.

Finally, 'If a customer returns any items, they are added back into stock and the copy of the delivery note is altered accordingly'. There are no new entities here. The first part of this is straightforward, Customer returns Item, and could be modelled as in Figure 7.12.

Figure 7.10

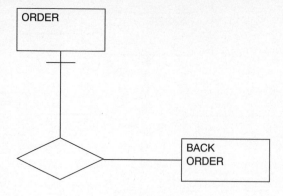

Figure 7.11

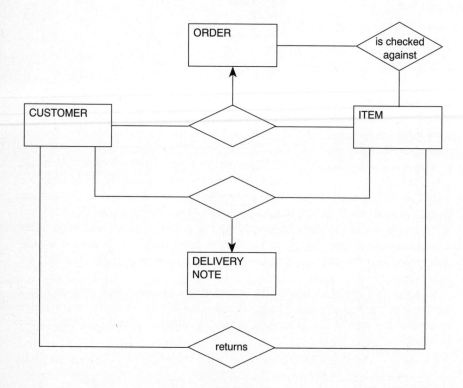

Figure 7.12

This takes care of items being added into stock, but not the alteration of the Delivery Note. This is a situation where the relationship could connect more

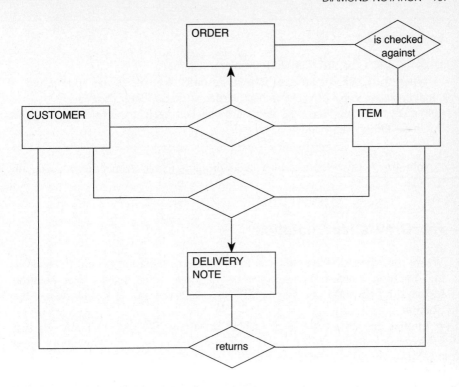

Figure 7.13

than two entities, because returns also cause Delivery Notes to be adjusted. So, the diagram could be completed as in Figure 7.13.

The last thing to do is to look at the diagram and consider each pair of entities for missing relationships. The only pair of entities not directly connected are Order and Delivery Note. While each order will eventually result in a Delivery Note, there appears to be no direct relationship between the two entities, so the diagram remains the same.

So, what have we learnt from that example? Well, we saw how nouns and verbs in the problem statement can help to identify potential entities and relationships, but there still needs to be a lot of consideration before deciding to model them on the diagram. In particular, we don't draw entities on the diagram for objects with no stored data, for example the catalogue or the Back Orders file. Also, we saw that relationships may have stored data of their own, for example Orders and Delivery Notes. These may then have separate relationships with other entities. Finally, we saw that relationships may connect more than two entities.

Exercise 7.1

Draw an ERD for the following problem statement.

When the stock for an item is low, an order is made to the appropriate supplier and a copy of the Purchase Order is filed. When there are deliveries from suppliers, the items are checked against the relevant Purchase Orders, and added to stock.

A solution to this exercise is walked through in the Appendix, starting on p. 211.

7.4 'Crow's feet' notation

We've now seen an example of an ERD using the diamond notation as used in the Yourdon method. Let's move on to look at the crow's feet notation favoured by SSADM and Gane and Sarson and see how it would change the example.

Entities are almost the same in both notations. The only difference is that sub-types are drawn differently. For example, rather than drawing sub-types as we did in the diamond notation (see Figure 7.2), they would now be drawn as in Figure 7.14.

Relationships are quite different though. The diamond is lost altogether and the relationship is now the line between the entities. This means that we lose the concept of associative object types and relationships connecting more than

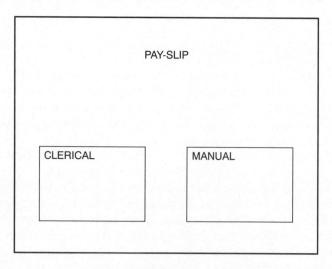

Figure 7.14

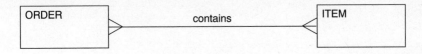

Figure 7.15

two entities. However, the gain is that cardinality is shown for each relationship. This shows whether one or a number of the occurrences of the connected entities participate in the relationship. This gives rise to three different types of relationship: many to many, one to many, and one to one. Let's have a look at an example of each of these in turn.

A many to many relationship would be drawn as in Figure 7.15 with a crow's foot at each end. This relationship could now be read 'Each order contains many items and each item appears on many orders'. It's well accepted that it is important to read these relationships in both directions and some argue that two names should appear on the relationship as in Figure 7.16. It is important to emphasize again that we're talking about object types rather than real-world objects. So, the Item entity here is referring to items in general, not to a particular tin of baked beans.

A one to many relationship would be drawn as in Figure 7.17 with a crow's foot only at the 'many' end. This reads 'each customer places many orders and each order is placed by one customer'.

A one to one relationship would be drawn as in Figure 7.18 with no crow's feet. This reads 'each project is led by one project leader and each project

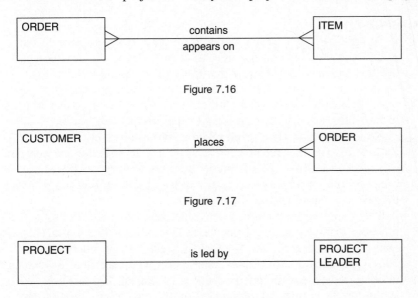

Figure 7.16

Figure 7.17

Figure 7.18

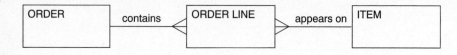

Figure 7.19

leader leads one project'. This gives us some useful information, for example we know that a project is never led by two people jointly and we know that a project leader is never leading two projects at the same time. However, it's generally accepted that entities connected by one to one relationships could be combined. In this case, project leader could become an attribute of the project entity.

It's also fairly well accepted now that each many to many relationship should be reduced to two one to many relationships if this is possible. This can often be accomplished by identifying and removing a repeating group from one of the entities. If we look back at the example in Figure 7.16, a many to many relationship between Order and Item, we can see that there might be a repeating group in the Order entity. There could be some static information for each order, like order number and date, but also a repeating group of item number, quantity, etc. for each item ordered. This could be removed and modelled as an entity for an Order Line, i.e. an item line on a particular order. This could be added to our model as in Figure 7.19. This reads 'Each order contains many order lines and each order line appears on one order. Each item appears on many order lines and each order line is one item.'

EXAMPLE 7.2

Let's see how this notation works in practice. If we go back to our example in the diamond notation, to change this to the crow's feet notation we must first redraw it without the diamond relationship symbols, as in Figure 7.20. Notice that the former associative object types have now become full entities. They have a relationship to each of the entities that were connected to the original relationship.

Now, let's think about each relationship in turn and consider cardinality. The first relationship that we'll look at is the one between Customer and Order. This is probably a one to many relationship because each customer places many orders, but each order is placed by only one customer (see Figure 7.21).

There are two relationships between Order and Item. Both are probably many to many. In one case, each order is checked against many items, and each item is checked against many orders. In the other case, each order contains many items, and each item is contained in many orders. Really, one of these is redundant. If you think about it, the former is more like a process on the data than a relationship between two entities, so we'll get rid of it. Also, we want to try to

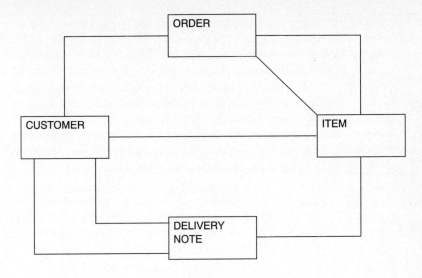

Figure 7.20

reduce the remaining many to many relationship to two one to many relationships. In this case, we can take out a repeating group from Order and introduce an Order Line entity, similar to the one that we saw earlier in Figure 7.19. This now reads 'each order contains many order lines, and each order line relates to one order; each item is

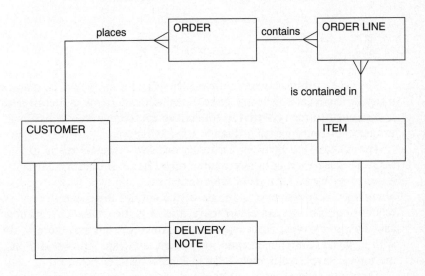

Figure 7.21

contained in many order lines, and each order line relates to one order'. This results in a partially converted ERD as in Figure 7.21.

If we look at the entities Customer and Delivery Note now, we again have two relationships. These are both one to many. In the first case each customer receives many Delivery Notes, but each Delivery Note is sent to only one customer. In the second case, each customer amends many Delivery Notes, but each Delivery Note is amended by only one customer. Again, we only need one of these to express the relationship between the entities rather than the processes carried out on them. So, we'll get rid of one as in Figure 7.22.

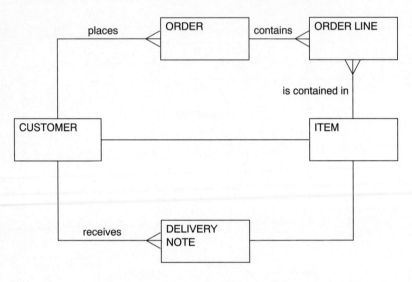

Figure 7.22

The relationship between Delivery Note and Item would be many to many because each Delivery Note contains many items and each item is contained in many Delivery Notes. We can reduce this to two one to many relationships as in Figure 7.23, as before.

The relationship between Customer and Item is again many to many because each customer returns many items and each item is returned by many customers. This time there's no neat way of removing a sub-structure from one of the entities to reduce the relationship. So, we can either leave it as it is, or create what's known as a link entity type, as in Figure 7.24. However, this has more to do with a physical implementation model and, as we're still working at the logical level, we'll leave it as in Figure 7.25 for now.

There are several points to note with our new model. We've now lost associative object types, so it is not as obvious what is ongoing

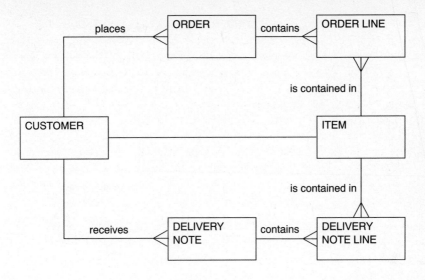

Figure 7.23

(or persistent) data and what is transaction data. However, their removal did point up some redundant relationships that weren't needed in the model. All relationships now connect only two entities, but this doesn't diminish our model in any way. We've now recorded cardinality for each relationship. This is useful information, even though it takes a lot of muttering to arrive at. But more than that, it

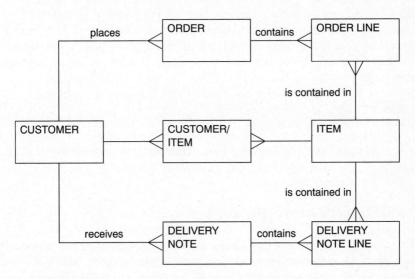

Figure 7.24

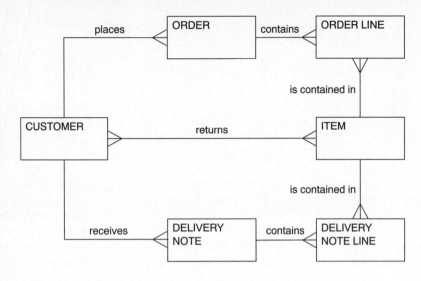

Figure 7.25

shows where we might want to combine entities and where we might want to create new entities. This moves us a step towards the eventual physical implementation of the database.

Exercise 7.2

Draw an ERD in the crow's feet notation for the problem statement in Exercise 7.1 (repeated below). You can either start from scratch or base it on the diagram in the diamond notation that you developed previously.

When the stock for an item is low, an order is made to the appropriate supplier and a copy of the Purchase Order is filed. When there are deliveries from suppliers, the items are checked against the relevant Purchase Orders, and added to stock.

A solution to this exercise is walked through in the Appendix, starting on p.214.

7.5 DFD–ERD correspondence

We've seen how to develop ERDs in both the diamond and crow's feet notations. As was mentioned at the start of the chapter, there are many variations and advanced features to both notations, but we'll just stick to the basics here. Before we leave the subject, though, it is worth considering the tie-up between ERDs and DFDs and what we would record in the data dictionary for entities and relationships.

First, the link between ERDs and DFDs. This is worth considering as both a consistency and a completeness check, and to help in developing one type of diagram when the other already exists. Yourdon's rule for the link between the two types of diagram is that there should be a one to one correspondence between the entities on the ERD and the data stores on the DFD. This might work for the diamond notation adopted by Yourdon if you don't count associative object types as entities, but it is probably too simplistic for ERDs drawn with the crow's feet notation.

Consider the DFD for college applications in Figure 7.26. Obviously, the stores could be entities, but what about the other parts of the diagram? Let's think about the external entities. Well, we might want to store data about graduates, so Graduate could be a valid addition to our entity model. The flow from Graduate, Application, seems like an even safer bet for an entity. The distinction between Application and Applications Book could be that the former contains information from the actual application, while the latter contains information about the progress of the application, e.g. when it was received, when references were requested. Presumably, graduates could apply for more than one postgraduate course, so we could model this on our ERD as in Figure 7.27.

Here each graduate sends many applications and each application is sent by one graduate. If we find an external entity on the DFD that we want to be an entity on the ERD, it probably indicates that the DFD is incomplete. In this case, it probably means that there ought to be a Graduate data store. This is not unexpected, and one of the benefits of having more than one perspective is that it highlights omissions and inconsistencies and leads to a more complete and correct model of the system. It is possible that the DFD might highlight problems with the ERD as well as the other way round.

It is less clear that data flows that we want to be entities represent a problem. When we first looked at DFDs we characterized data stores as background or persistent data, often embodied in databases or master files. Data flows were characterized as transactions that might be embodied in transaction files. It is clear from our study of entities that they could be of either type. In the diamond notation, a distinction is made between the two types, with persistent data modelled as entities and transaction data modelled as associative object types. No such distinction is made in the crow's feet notation.

Continuing with our example, we might want to store some data about referees, and Referee might be added to our model as in Figure 7.28. This again would highlight a problem with the DFD. On the ERD, the relationship between Referee and Application would be many to many because each referee appears on many applications and each application contains many referees.

If we now consider some of the other flows, Reference might be something that we would want to store data about, and this could be added to the entity

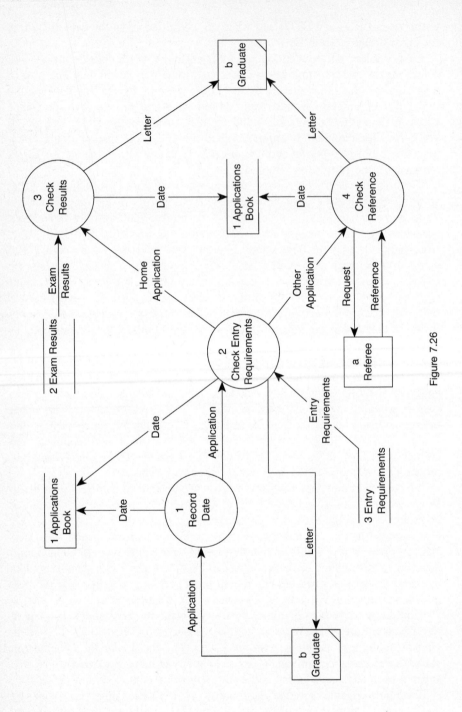

Figure 7.26

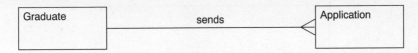

Figure 7.27

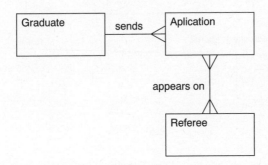

Figure 7.28

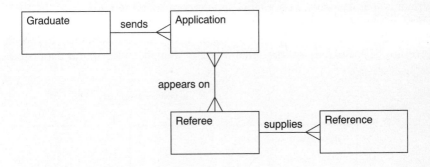

Figure 7.29

model as in Figure 7.29. Because each Referee could supply a reference for more than one graduate, the relationship is 'each referee supplies many references and each reference is supplied by one referee'. Similarly, Home Applications and Other Applications might be useful additions to our entity model. These could be modelled as sub-types of Application as in Figure 7.30. We won't worry about the cardinality here, but each home application is checked against exam results and each other application requires a reference.

Finally, the processes on the DFD won't give us any help with the entities, but they might correspond to some of the relationships. For example, we can

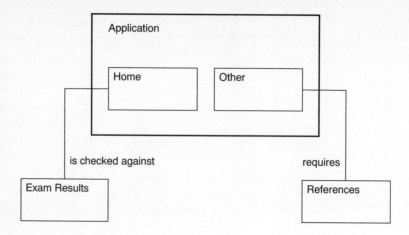

Figure 7.30

see that the processes on the DFD for checking entry requirements, exam results and references could be reflected in the relationships on the ERD as in Figure 7.31.

So, the link between DFDs and ERDs is not clear-cut. All we can say for certain is that data stores on a DFD should correspond to entities on the ERD. There might also be some correspondence between the external entities and data flows on a DFD and the entities on an ERD, at least initially. This would have to be resolved on the final model, though, with extra data stores

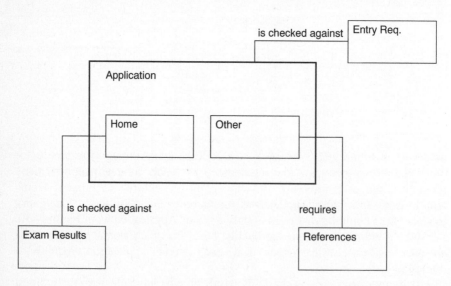

Figure 7.31

introduced, because Yourdon requires a 1:1 correspondence between data stores and entities, and SSADM requires a 1:N correspondence. The processes might correspond to some of the relationships.

7.6 Data dictionary

When we've got an ERD that we're happy with, what should we record in the data dictionary? Well, entities and relationships could be recorded in a similar way to data stores and data flows. That is, for entities, the data dictionary should automatically capture connected relationships, and allow the attributes to be recorded. For relationships, the data dictionary should automatically capture connected entities. In the diamond notation, which has the concept of relationships having data via associative object types, there might also be the facility to record attributes. In the crow's feet notation, this isn't necessary.

One addition to the data dictionary needed for entities is a way of identifying a key, that is, a unique identifier for the entity made up of one or more attributes. Yourdon suggests that key attributes could be prefixed with an @.

7.7 ERD summary

This concludes our look at ERDs. We've seen how to construct ERDs using both the diamond notation favoured by Yourdon and the crow's feet used by SSADM and Gane and Sarson. We've also considered the correspondence between DFDs and ERDs and what we should record in the data dictionary for entities and relationships.

ERDs show how to construct a high-level data-orientated view of a system that parallels the process-orientated view presented in the DFD. These two graphical views, together with the underlying data dictionary, give a comprehensive logical model of the system. This completes our study of 'top-down' data modelling and we will now move on to look at how we might model data 'bottom-up' using data normalization.

7.8 Data normalization

The data parts of our model are entity relationship diagrams, and data flows and data stores from data flow diagrams. The process of moving from this logical representation towards a physical implementation may be approached top-down or bottom-up.

The top-down approach is usually applied to ERDs, particularly when moving towards a relational database. Here a process generally referred to as attribution is carried out, where the attributes (or data elements) are assigned to entities. As this proceeds, entities may be split or combined. This might be just to remove one to one or many to many relationships, or to fit in with the physical implementation. This is the approach adopted by Yourdon. From our work with ERDs earlier, we can imagine how this might proceed.

However, the other approach, bottom-up, is new to us and we'll spend some time looking at it here. This is a well-known process called normalization. It could be applied to entities (with attributes) or data stores (with data elements). Gane and Sarson propose that normalization be applied to data stores. This is logical, because when defining the structure of data stores we identify iterations, and this is useful when performing normalization. However, with a little extra work, it could be applied equally well to entities. SSADM utilizes an approach to data modelling that incorporates both entity relationship diagrams and data normalization.

Normalization is a way of taking raw, or unnormalized, data and splitting it into smaller, simpler groupings of data. These groupings of data are often called relations or tables. The object of the exercise is to come up with a flexible and maintainable data implementation. As with the top-down approach, it has been used particularly with relational databases.

An alternative title for normalization is 'inspired common sense'. This is appropriate because the process of normalization is one that good data designers carry out intuitively. It's a three-step process taking the data from unnormalized form through first and second to third normal form.

The process starts with unnormalized data. That is, for an entity we have identified its attributes; and for a data store we have identified its data elements and data structures. For data stores, we are only really interested in the data elements, although any iteration structures are also of interest.

Now, let's look at an example to illustrate this process.

EXAMPLE 7.3

We might have a manual file of customer orders as in Figure 7.32. At the top of each order there is some information that occurs only once per order: a customer number, name and address, a date and a salesman number and name. Below that is a line for each item

ORDER

Date :

Customer No :

Salesman
No :
Name :

Name   :
Address   :

Item No.	Description	Quantity	Price
		Order Value	

Figure 7.32

ordered, made up of an item number and description, a quantity and a price. This is a repeating group. At the bottom we have the total order value. This could be written down as unnormalized data:

```
Order (Customer No, Date, Cust Name, Cust
        Address, Salesman No, Salesman Name,
        (Item No, Description, Quantity, Price),
        Order Value)
```

There are several points to notice here. First, the relation has been given a name, Order. This could be any name that describes the whole relation. Second, all the attributes of the relation are listed and enclosed in brackets. The order of the attributes is not important at this stage. Third, any repeating groups are enclosed in brackets of their own within the main brackets. This means that any repeating groups must be identified at the outset, even before writing down the data in unnormalized form.

To move to first normal form, we first need to identify a key for the whole relation, and a key for each repeating group. A key is an attribute, or combination of attributes, that acts as a unique identifier. We then remove the repeating groups.

So, if we first consider the key for the whole relation, the customer number on its own isn't enough to uniquely identify an order because, over a period of time, a customer may make many orders. If we assume that customers never order more than once a day, the key could be customer number and date. For the repeating group, item number will do as the key. That is, item number is enough to uniquely identify a particular occurrence of the repeating group for a particular order. It's usual to underline the key attributes as follows:

```
Order (Customer No, Date, Cust Name, Cust
        Address, Salesman No, Salesman Name,
        (Item No, Description, Quantity, Price),
        Order Value)
```

The repeating group then needs to be removed:

```
Order (Cust No, Date, Cust Name, Cust Address,
       Salesman No, Salesman Name, Order Value)
Order-Item (Cust No, Date, Item No,
                    Description, Quantity, Price)
```

Notice that the repeating group has now gone completely from the original relation, Order, to form a new relation of its own, Order-Item. Also, the key of Order (Customer Number and Date) is removed along with the repeating group to help form the key of the new relation. This maintains the link between an order and its items and still allows an order item to be uniquely identified. The data is now in first normal form.

To move to second normal form, we need to remove partial key dependencies. That is, we need to identify non-key attributes that are dependent on only part of the key and remove them together with that part of the key. So, let's look for this in Order and Order Item in the above data structure. In Order, Salesman Number and Name, and Order Value, are dependent on the whole key so they stay put. That is, the three attributes are not dependent on just Customer Number, or Date, but on the combination of them. Customer Name and Address are only dependent on Customer Number, so they could be removed together with the part of the key that they depend on to make a new relation. In Order Item, quantity is dependent on the whole key, but description and price are only dependent on item number, so they can be removed. The following data is now in second normal form.

```
Order (Cust No, Date, Salesman No,
       Salesman Name, Order Value)
Customer (Cust No, Cust Name, Cust Address)
Order-Item (Cust No, Date, Item No, Quantity)
Item (Item No, Description, Price)
```

Notice that while the attributes with partial key dependencies disappear from the original relation to appear in the new relation, the partial key appears in both. For example, Customer Name and Address disappear from Order and appear in Customer, while Customer Number appears in Customer and also stays in Order. This is partly to maintain links, as before, but also because we must not disturb the key of the original relation. For example, if we took Customer Number out of Order along with Customer Name and Address, we would be left with a key of Date in Order. This doesn't make sense because we would expect more than one order in a day. Notice also that the partial key removed with the attributes with partial key dependencies becomes the key of the new relation, e.g. Customer Number is now the key of Customer. Relations with simple keys (i.e. one attribute) need not be considered for partial key dependencies because there are no parts to the key.

To move to third normal form, we must remove non-key dependencies. That is, we need to identify non-key attributes that depend on other non-key attributes and remove them. There could be non-key dependencies in Order, Customer or Item (there couldn't in Order-Item because there is only one non-key attribute). If we look at Item, there is no dependency between Description and Price, and very little relationship, apart from the fact that they both depend on Item Number. In Customer, Customer Address appears to depend on Customer Name, but when we think about it more, they are already in a relation called Customer and the real dependence is each of them on the key of the relation, Customer Number. In Order, there appears to be a similar dependence between Salesman Number and Name. This time, though, the attributes are not in a relation to do with salesmen, nor do they depend on anything to do with salesmen. Here, Salesman Name is dependent on Salesman Number, so we should remove them both. Notice that the key of the new relation is Salesman Number, and that this also remains in the original relation to make the link.

```
Order (Cust No, Date, Salesman No,
          Order Value)
Customer (Cust No, Cust Name, Cust Address)
Order-Item (Cust No, Date, Item No, Quantity)
Item (Item No, Description, Price)
Salesman (Salesman No, Salesman Name)
```

So, we end up with five relations. Obviously, we could draw an ERD from this quite simply using either of the notations that we looked at earlier. Each relation in third normal form could be an entity on the ERD.

A common criticism of normalization is that it breaks down the data too far and, if this is implemented directly, database performance will be poor. Obviously, although normalization provides us with useful guidelines, it must be tempered by practical considerations.

We might summarize the normalization process as follows:

1. Write down the unnormalized data, identifying any repeating groups in brackets.
2. Choose a key for the whole relation and for any repeating groups.

3. Remove any repeating groups together with the main key.
4. Identify and remove any partial key dependencies.
5. Identify and remove any non-key dependencies.

Obviously, there is a good deal of human intelligence in this process, and it could never be made completely automatic. However, it can be supported by a CASE tool.

Exercise 7.3

Normalize the data in the Time Sheet in Figure 7.33.

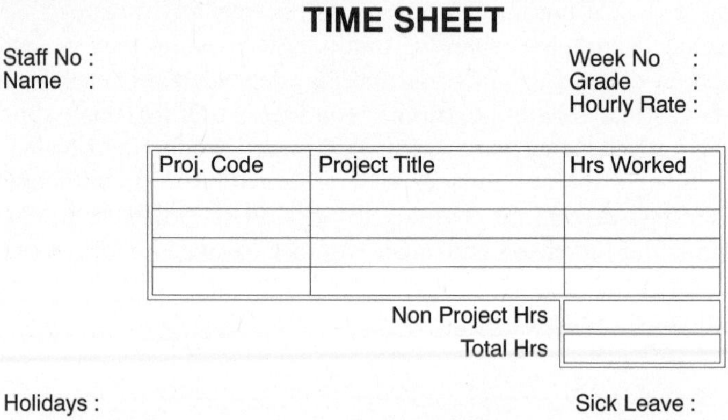

TIME SHEET

Staff No :   Week No   :
Name   :   Grade   :
                                                    Hourly Rate :

Proj. Code	Project Title	Hrs Worked

	Non Project Hrs	
	Total Hrs	

Holidays :   Sick Leave :

Figure 7.33

A solution to this exercise is walked through in the Appendix, starting on p. 218.

7.9 Data modelling summary

In this chapter we've looked at two approaches to data modelling: entity relationship diagrams and data normalization. We now have two perspectives on the system that we are modelling: process and data. In the next chapter, we will go on to look at a third perspective that we might consider: time, or behaviour.

CHAPTER 8

Entity life histories

8.1 Introduction

So far we have been concentrating on the techniques that model computer-based systems from two perspectives: process and data. We have seen how data flow diagrams and parts of the data dictionary can give us a process-based perspective, and how entity relationship diagrams, data normalization and other parts of the data dictionary can give us a data-based perspective.

Many people would argue that to get a complete and consistent model of a system requires a third perspective: time, or behaviour. That is, not only do we need to model the processes and data of the system in a static way, we must also model how the processes and data behave over time.

SSADM was one of the first methods to incorporate this third perspective using the technique of entity life histories (ELHs), and it is these that we will concentrate on for most of this chapter. To support this work on ELHs, we will be taking a look at how to recognize events and how to construct entity event matrices.

The Yourdon method also proposes a technique for modelling the time perspective: state transition diagrams (STDs). These are most often used in the Yourdon method as a way of exploding extended DFDs when modelling real-time systems. This is beyond the scope of this book, but STDs can be used independently for modelling the behavioural perspective of information systems, and towards the end of the chapter we will spend some time looking at how this could be done.

8.2 Entity life histories

As the name suggests, this technique concentrates on the life history of entities. That is, for each entity that we have previously identified (on the ERD) we consider how it behaves over time, i.e. how it might be created, how it might be modified through its life, and how it might be deleted. For example, if we were considering an Applications entity in a university admissions system, it might be created upon initial receipt of the application; it might be modified when results were checked, when references were requested and received, and when an offer or decline was sent out; and it might be deleted if the application was declined, if the student declined the offer, or when the student enrolled on the course. Unlike the ERD for the system, or the set of DFDs, we would expect there to be a number of separate ELHs when we have finished modelling: one for each entity.

8.3 Events

In considering each entity, we are interested in each event in the system that affects the entity. It is important to distinguish between events and effects here, because it is the events that we are interested in, at least initially. An event is an occurrence that triggers a change to an entity. The change to the entity is the effect. For example, a student applying for a course is an event, and the creation of an Application record is the effect. Similarly, requesting a reference is an event, and recording the date that the reference was requested on the Application record is the effect.

In SSADM, there are thought to be three types of event:

- Externally generated
- Internally recognized, and
- Time-based.

Externally generated events are those that are generated from outside the system, like a student sending in an application. Internally recognized events are those that are recognized inside the system, like stock falling below a reorder level. Time-based events are those that are triggered by time, like monthly invoicing or chasing requests for references after a month.

Yourdon also believes that there are three types of event, but these are not the same three as in SSADM. They are:

- Flow-orientated
- Temporal, and
- Control.

Control events only generally appear in real-time systems and so may be disregarded here. Temporal events are like time-based events in SSADM. Flow-orientated events are those that are associated with data flows and so are somewhat similar to externally generated events in SSADM.

So, we have in mind what an event is, and what types of event there might be, and this is important in identifying a complete set of events, but how do we go about it practically? A good starting point for this is the DFD because it clearly shows which processes affect which data stores.

There should be a correspondence between entities on the ERD and data stores on the DFD, as we saw in the previous chapter. Therefore, using the DFD, it is simple to see effects (i.e. changes to entities). These would merely be data stores with a data flow coming into them. These could then be traced

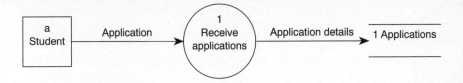

Figure 8.1

back to find the events (i.e. the occurrences that triggered the changes to the entities). Note that the process updating the data store is not necessarily the event (although it could be!). The process might have more to do with the effect than the event, or it might be dealing with several events.

Let's look at some examples of this. In Figure 8.1, a student sends in an application, which is received, with the application details going to create an application record in the Applications store. We know that there is an effect here because we can see the data flow into the Applications data store. If we trace back, we find the event, which we might describe as 'student applies' or 'application received'. This is an externally generated event.

In Figure 8.2, after entry requirements have been checked, a reference is requested and the date of the request is recorded in the Applications data store. The effect is the update of the store and the event could be written 'reference requested'. This is an internally recognized event because nothing external has triggered it. The event has not been recognized because something has happened to the data but because it has a certain place in the internal procedures.

In Figure 8.3, we can see an internally recognized event that is recognized because of something that has happened to the data. When stock is adjusted, it is noticed that it has gone below the reorder level, resulting in a Requisition Note to Purchasing, with a copy being filed (the effect). The event here could be written as 'stock low' or 'stock falls below reorder level'.

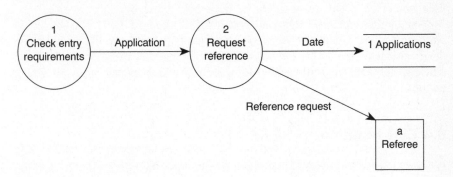

Figure 8.2

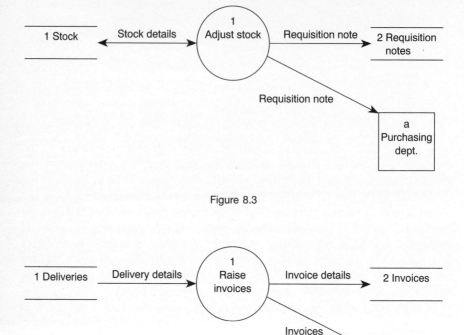

Figure 8.3

Figure 8.4

In Figure 8.4, we can see a time-based event. Once a month, delivery details are used to raise invoices, which are sent to the customer, with a copy being filed (the effect). The event might be written as 'raise monthly invoices'.

You might remember that one way of developing a DFD was by event partitioning (see Chapter 4, section 4.4). This uses an event list to drive the development of the DFD. Obviously, an event list is extremely useful here, although the DFD is still needed to work out which events apply to which entities.

8.4 ELH notation

Having identified the events that relate to an entity, the next step is to develop the ELH. Before we go on to look at an example, let's first take a look at the notation. ELHs are a graphical technique using the well-established notation of

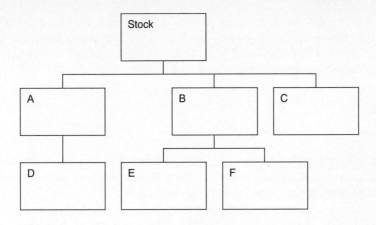

Figure 8.5

Jackson structure diagrams. We are well acquainted with the notions of sequence, selection and iteration from our look at data dictionaries in Chapters 5 and 6. There we saw how these notions applied to data and process. Here we are interested in applying sequence, selection and iteration to the events that affect an entity over the course of its life. The key difference is that this time we will be using a graphical rather than a textual notation.

ELHs are drawn as inverted trees with the name of the entity in the 'root node', as in Figure 8.5. The other nodes in the tree (the rectangular boxes) might be thought of as either 'leaf nodes' or 'structure nodes'. Leaf nodes occur at the end of branches and contain the name of the event that affects the entity. In Figure 8.5, nodes D, E, F and C are leaf nodes. Any other nodes (i.e. those that have subordinates) are structure nodes. In Figure 8.5, nodes A and B are structure nodes. These are not events but merely structuring mechanisms that allow us to define the relationship of the leaf nodes (events) using sequence, selection and iteration.

We show a sequence in ELHs in Figure 8.6. Here node A is decomposed into a sequence: B, followed by C, followed by D. The way that we draw the

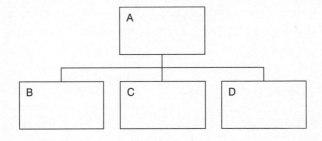

Figure 8.6

nodes left to right across the page to denote a sequence is similar to how we wrote data elements (or statements) down the page to denote a sequence in the data dictionary. For example, if A, B, C and D were data, we would write the above structure in the data dictionary as follows:

A
  B
  C
  D

B, C and D are indented from A to show that they are its decomposition and are written in the order of their sequence. Note the similarity of data elements to leaf nodes, and of data structures to structure nodes.

Because the sequence is drawn left to right on an ELH, it is worth noting that the generic shape of any ELH should be as in Figure 8.7. That is, the generic life history of any entity may be decomposed into its birth, followed by its life, followed by its death. This sounds staggeringly obvious, but many people do not realize it when they first encounter ELHs. Obviously, the birth, life and death parts are likely to be decomposed into more complicated sub-structures, but it is important to realize that we will find the events that deal with the creation of an entity on the left of an ELH, and those that deal with its modification and deletion in the middle and on the right, respectively.

We show selection in ELHs in Figure 8.8. Here node A is decomposed into either node B or node C, but not into both. The selection nodes are identified by an O in the top right-hand corner. Perhaps this was meant to stand for 'or' originally? Whether this is true or not, it is useful to think of these nodes as 'OR nodes'.

A special case of selection in ELHs uses the 'null node' as in Figure 8.9. Here, node A is decomposed into either node B or nothing. This can be seen as a parallel to the way that we wished to identify optional data elements in the data dictionary.

We show iteration in ELHs in Figure 8.10. Here, node A is decomposed into an iteration of node B. Iteration is shown as an asterisk in the top right-hand corner of the box. Strictly, iteration means that there will be zero or more

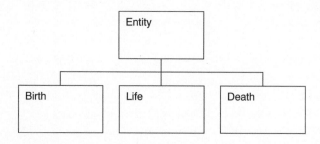

Figure 8.7

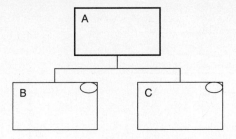

Figure 8.8

occurrences, so this too could cover a type of optionality. Notice again the similarity with the data part of the data dictionary, where an asterisk is also used to denote iteration.

So, that is how the notation for sequence, selection and iteration is used in ELHs in isolation, but we obviously want to put them all together to draw a complete ELH. The rule for combining the structures is simple. Any node may be decomposed into either sequence, selection or iteration, but not into a combination of these. That is, sequence, selection and iteration must not be mixed on the same level of the same branch of the tree. Let's take a look at some examples to clarify this.

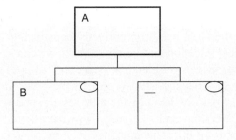

Figure 8.9

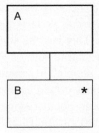

Figure 8.10

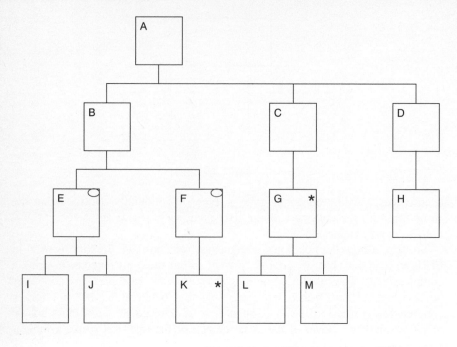

Figure 8.11

In Figure 8.11 the ELH has been correctly constructed. We can see all the structures: sequence, selection and iteration. Also, we can see different types of decomposition: sequence to selection, selection to sequence, selection to iteration, iteration to sequence, and so on. All these decompositions are quite valid. If we look across one level of the tree, say the nodes E, F, G and H, we can see selection, iteration and sequence. However, there is no problem with this as they all occur on different branches. The problem comes when a node is decomposed into a mixture of sequence, selection or iteration, as in Figure 8.12. Here, what is meant is that node A is decomposed into node X or node Y, followed by node Z. This mixture of selection and sequence in a single decomposition is not allowed. The way to draw this is as in Figure 8.13.

Now, node A is decomposed into node B followed by node Z, where node B is either node X or node Y. This has the same meaning as was intended in Figure 8.12, but preserves the simple rule of the diagramming notation. This simplicity is attractive: many people in computing having learnt from bitter experience the value of the KISS principle (Keep It Simple, Stupid).

Now we have seen how to go about recognizing events from a DFD, and how events might be structured on an ELH using sequence, selection and iteration, it's time to look at an example of how an ELH could be constructed.

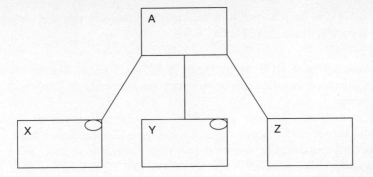

Figure 8.12

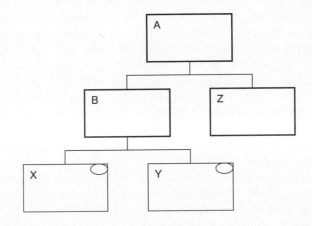

Figure 8.13

EXAMPLE 8.1

In Chapter 2 we looked at how to draw a DFD for a college applications system (see Example 2.1). The problem statement was as follows.

A college processes applications for its postgraduate courses from home graduates and those from other institutions. The Admissions section records the date of receipt of all applications in the Applications Book. Home graduates are accepted if they meet the entry requirements (this is also checked against lists of previous examination results by the Records section). Other graduates are rejected if they don't meet the entry requirements, and even if they do, a reference is sought. If this is satisfactory, the graduate is accepted. All applicants receive a letter from the college advising them if they've been accepted or rejected, and the date that this is sent is recorded in the Applications Book.

This resulted in a DFD as in Figure 8.14. You might like to review the development of that DFD from the problem statement in Chapter 2 before continuing.

Let us now consider how we would go about constructing an ELH from this scenario for the entity Applications Book. (We will assume that there is a one to one correspondence between the data store Applications Book and an entity of the same name on the ERD.) As we said earlier, a good starting point for this is the DFD because it will clearly show us the effects on the entity. This will allow us to trace the events that caused the effects, and these are important because they are going to be modelled on the ELH.

Let's have a look for effects on the Applications Book on the DFD and try to identify the events. The first effect is the date written to the Applications Book from the first process 'Record Application'. The event that has caused this is the applicant sending in an application form. This is the creation event for the entity, i.e. we will only have entries in the Applications Book once we have applications. The labelling of the data flow on the DFD does not make this clear. In fact, it sounds as if a date of receipt is just being added to a pre-existing record. In retrospect, 'Application Details' would have been a better label for the flow than 'Date'. It is just this sort of imprecision, together with more important inconsistencies and omissions, that we are trying to pick up by modelling from a third perspective.

The next effect is the date written to the Applications Book from the second process 'Check Entry Requirements'. The event here is not the entry requirements check because we are not updating the Applications Book with the date that we did that check. The event is the sending of the rejection letter.

The next effect is the date written to the Applications Book when a letter is sent from the third process 'Check Results'. Like the previous effect, the event here is not the results check but the sending of the letter.

The last effect is the date written to the Applications Book when a letter is sent from the fourth process 'Check References'. The event is again the sending of the letter. Just to make the example a little more interesting, let's say that there are another two events hiding in here. Let's say that dates are also added to the Applications Book when references are requested and when references are received. That gives us another two events: references requested and references received. (This doesn't require a change to the DFD, at least not at the top level that we are looking at.)

Having thought about the effects on the Applications Book on the DFD, and the events that caused them, we could now draw up an event list. The simplest event list would be as follows:

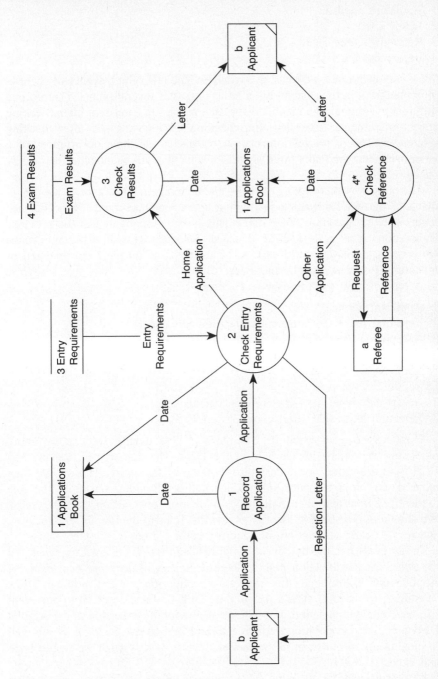

Figure 8.14

1. Applicant applies.
2. Letter sent.
3. References requested.
4. References received.

We could elaborate on event 2 in two ways. The other three events all occur at only one point in the system, but a letter is sent at several points. Therefore, a different event could be identified for each point, i.e. letter sent after checking entry requirements, letter sent after checking results, letter sent after checking references. This is useful information because these three occurrences of a letter being sent are really three separate events that will be modelled separately on the ELH.

The other way that event 2 could be elaborated is to specify the type of letter that is being sent. Rather than just saying 'letter sent', we could say 'acceptance letter sent' or 'rejection letter sent'. This is less important than the previous elaboration as it is less clear that we are dealing with different events. However, a decision would have to be made based on the level or detail of modelling that was thought necessary.

A longer event list could be as follows:

1. Applicant applies.
2. Rejection letter sent after entry requirements check.
3. Acceptance letter sent after results check.
4. Rejection letter sent after results check.
5. References requested.
6. References received.
7. Acceptance letter sent after references checked.
8. Rejection letter sent after references checked.

Now we have an event list (in more or less detail), we can set about modelling the ELH with the help of the DFD. The first step in drawing any ELH is to draw the root node with the name of the entity. This should then break down into a sequence of birth, life and death nodes. We should be able to identify events that refer to the birth, or creation, of occurrences of the entity. We should also be able to identify events that refer to the life, or modification, and to the death, or deletion, of occurrences of the entity.

In our event list, the first event 'Applicant applies' is the creation event. All the others are modification events. There is no way of deleting occurrences of Applications Book, and this reflects an omission on the original DFD. Therefore, we need to extend the original DFD and add an event to our event list that deals with deletion. We will not deal with the extension to the original DFD here, beyond pointing out that the third perspective is doing its job well in picking up an omission in the model. This is exactly what we would hope and expect.

Concerning adding an event to deal with deletion, we have no information on the deletion of records from the Applications Book, so we will say that we

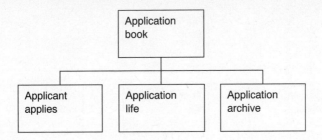

Figure 8.15

would not want to delete them completely from the system, but perhaps archive them from the Applications Book to a long-term store once a year. Thus, we could start our ELH as in Figure 8.15.

So, the life history of the entity Applications Book is a sequence of 'Applicant applies', followed by 'Application life', followed by 'Application archive'. The first and last of these are leaf nodes, or primitive events, and need not be decomposed further. The second, 'Application life', is a structure node and needs to be decomposed into the other primitive events for the entity.

Using the DFD, we can see that all applications go through the entry requirements check before being split into home applications and other applications. As all these processes contain events that affect our entity, the life history of the entity will follow a similar pattern. So, the structure node 'Application life' should be broken down into a sequence: 'Entry Requirements Check', followed by either 'Home Application Life' or 'Other Application Life'. It is tempting to draw this as in Figure 8.16.

However, the rules of the notation only allow us to decompose each node into either a sequence, selection or iteration, not a combination. Therefore, the next stage of our ELH should be as in Figure 8.17. Here, 'Application life' is decomposed into a sequence: 'Entry Requirements Check' followed by

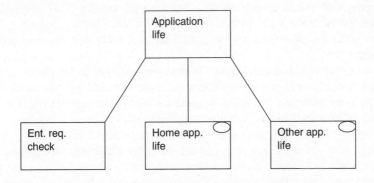

Figure 8.16

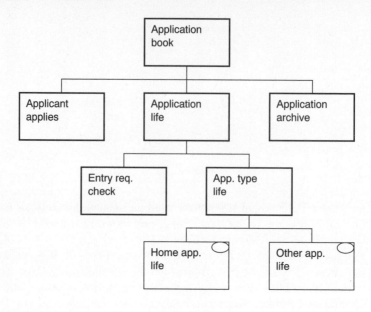

Figure 8.17

'Application Type Life'. 'Application Type Life' is then decomposed into a selection of either 'Home Application Life' or 'Other Application Life'.

This gives us the basic structure of the ELH. It is important to realize that this has been derived mostly from the DFD (and our knowledge of the expected layout of an ELH) rather than from the event list. This will often be the case. However, we do need to make progress with drawing the events on the ELH. We could do this either by going down the event list or by considering each of the new nodes on the diagram in turn. There isn't much to choose between these two methods, but we'll select the event list here.

The next event is the rejection letter sent after the entry requirements check. Obviously, the 'Entry Requirements Check' node on the ELH needs to be decomposed in some way. This is an optional event (nothing happens if the entry requirements are met), so we could use a selection with the null node as in Figure 8.18.

So, 'Entry Requirements Check' is decomposed into a selection: either a rejection letter is sent or nothing happens. If we decided not to model at the level of distinguishing between acceptance and rejection letters, the first selection node could just be labelled 'Letter sent'.

We will consider the next pair of events together – acceptance/rejection letter sent after results check. We can see from the DFD that the results check is only carried out for home applications, so it is the 'Home Applications Life' node that we want to decompose. This time the event is not an option. We know that we are always going to send an acceptance or rejection letter at this

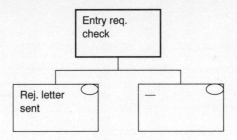

Figure 8.18

point. Therefore, the simplest decomposition of 'Home Application Life' is as in Figure 8.19. Here, the decomposition is into a sequence of one node 'Letter sent'. If we wanted more detail, we could break this node down further as in Figure 8.20. In fact, if we're going to do that we could lose the 'letter sent'

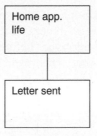

Figure 8.19

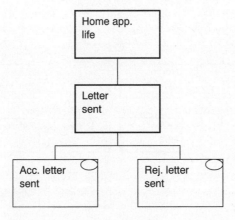

Figure 8.20

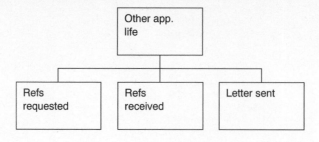

Figure 8.21

node altogether, as a sequence of one node isn't adding much to our model, but we'll continue without breaking the node down for simplicity.

The next four events are references requested, references received and acceptance/rejection letter sent after references are checked. These events all apply to the node 'Other Application Life', because we can see from the DFD that only Other Applications are input to the references check. We are dealing with a sequence here because references must be requested before they are received, and they must be received before a decision is made and an acceptance or rejection letter sent. This could be drawn as in Figure 8.21.

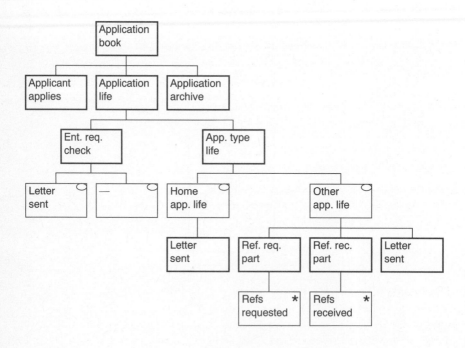

Figure 8.22

All these new nodes could be broken down further. If we assume that more than one reference will be requested, then we have an iteration. Similarly with 'References received'. 'Letter sent' could again be broken down into acceptance or rejection letter sent as in Figure 8.20. Our final ELH could look something like the one in Figure 8.22.

8.5 Entity event matrices

In the example, we have used our knowledge of ELHs, the DFD and an event list to construct the ELH. SSADM requires the construction of an entity event matrix (EEM) before any ELHs are drawn. This formalizes some of the points that we were considering above.

An EEM is a matrix of all the entities and all the events in a system. So, for the example that we have just been looking at, we could construct an EEM as in Table 8.1 Notice the list of events down the left-hand side and the names of all the entities across the top. When this basic matrix has been laid out, a C, M or D is entered into each cell. C stands for create, M for modify, and D for delete. So, for our example, 'Applicant applies' is the creation event, 'Application archived' is the deletion event, and the others are modification events. This would clearly point out before we starting drawing the ELH if we didn't have a particular type of event.

Table 8.1

	Applications Book	Entry Requirements	Exam Results
Applicant applies	C		
Letter sent	M		
References requested	M		
References received	M		
Apllication archive	D		

When all the cells have been completed, an ELH is drawn for each column (i.e. for each entity) in a similar way to the worked example above. SSADM also recommends that a diagram is drawn for each row on the EEM to trace the effects that each event has on all the entities. This is called an effect correspondence diagram, but we will not pursue its construction here as it is beyond the scope of the book.

Exercise 8.1

Orders are received from customers and validated against the Stock file to see if all the items exist. If they do not, the item is added to the stock file. Each order is then checked for availability. Orders that can be supplied

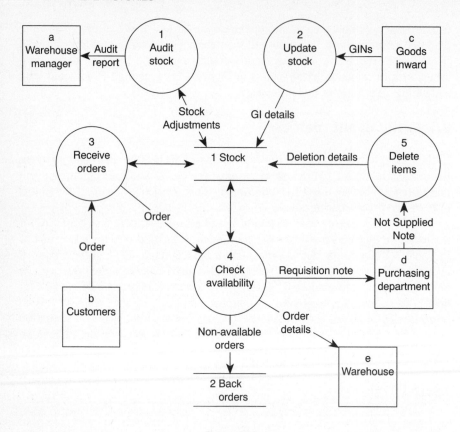

Figure 8.23

immediately have the order details sent to the warehouse and the Stock file
is decremented accordingly. Orders that cannot be satisfied immediately are
placed in a back orders file and a requisition note is sent to the Purchasing
Department for the missing items. If the items are no longer supplied, the
Purchasing Department sends back a Not Supplied note and the items are
deleted from the Stock file. When items are received from suppliers, the
Goods Inward Department completes a Goods Inward Note and the Stock
file is incremented. Once a year there is a stock audit which results in an
audit report to the warehouse manager. Any items not ordered in the last
year are deleted from the Stock file. Any items where there is a discrepancy
between the physical stock and the Stock file have their stock level adjusted
on the Stock file.

A DFD of this scenario is given in Figure 8.23.

Draw an entity life history for the Stock entity (assuming that there is an
entity Stock on the ERD that matches the Stock store on the DFD).

A solution to this exercise is walked through in the Appendix, starting on p. 220.

8.6 Advanced notations

The notations that we have looked at so far for ELHs will cope with the majority of situations that we want to model, but sometimes more advanced notations can be useful.

8.6.1 Parallel structure

There are occasions when drawing ELHs when we do not know the sequence of certain events. This might be simply that we cannot determine whether one event occurs before another. More common is the situation where the entity has a 'main life', but may be subject to a number of amendments during that life. For example, if we look back at our final ELH for the Applications Book in Figure 8.22, the 'Application Life' detailed there is the 'Main Life' of the entity. While this life is going on there might be any number of 'amendments', e.g. changes of name, address, referee, etc. But we don't know if the amendments will occur, or (if they do) at what point in the life history. In these situations we could use a parallel structure, as in Figure 8.24.

Here we have taken the first-level decomposition from our Applications Book example and decomposed the 'Application Life' node into a parallel structure, 'Main Life' and 'Amendments'. The sub-tree that was previously connected to 'Application Life' could now be connected to 'Main Life'. The structure of the amendments would be drawn using normal ELH notation and rules. However, while we might want to capture all these events eventually, there is a case for excluding anything but the main life, at least initially, because the amendments and exceptions can cloud the picture.

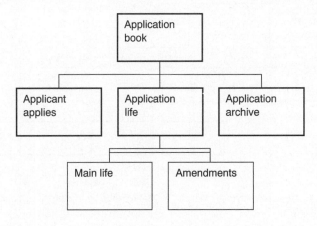

Figure 8.24

8.6.2 Quit and resume

In contrast to the orderly structures of sequence, selection and iteration normally found in ELHs, quit and resume is something like a GO TO statement in a programming language. Similarly, they should be avoided where possible, but there are some occasions when they might prove useful. If we go back to our Applications Book example again, we might find that students sometimes withdraw their applications while references are awaited. In this case we might want to go straight from the 'References requested' event to the 'Application archive' event without going through the rest of the normal life of the entity. This would be drawn as in Figure 8.25.

This notation means that in certain circumstances we want to quit the life history at 'References requested' and resume it at 'Application archive'. Q and R just stand for quit and resume. The '1' in both cases just identifies the quit and resume pair. If there was another quit and resume on the diagram they would be labelled Q2 and R2, and so on.

These situations might not be quite as simple as portrayed above. When exceptional circumstances arise, new events might need to be introduced into the ELH to deal with the exception. Also, it might raise the question of whether similar Quits might apply elsewhere on the ELH. In our example we have modelled the effect of a student withdrawing while waiting for references. Obviously, withdrawals could happen almost anywhere on the ELH. In these

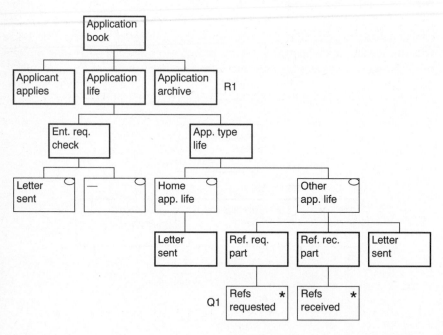

Figure 8.25

QUIT FROM ANYWHERE
TO R1 ON WITHDRAWAL

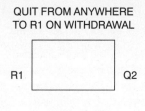

Figure 8.26

circumstances we can introduce a free-standing node into the ELH as in Figure 8.26. In this case we wouldn't put Q1's all over the diagram. This is covered by the generic phrase 'quit from anywhere'. The Q2 is then a GO TO to the deletion event on the main ELH, which will have R2 placed beside it.

Apart from their GO TO-ness, which has long been considered harmful in computing, as with parallel structures, too many quit and resumes on an ELH could obscure the main picture.

8.7 Operations

Operations on an ELH can be thought of as the effects on the entity. SSADM prescribes ten types of legal operations and gives some examples of illegal ones. We will not go into this in detail here, but the type of operations that we would be looking to add to our ELH would be to do with storing attributes (for the first time), replacing attributes (i.e. updating them) or maintaining relationships between entities. Operations are added to events as numbered boxes which refer to a separate, textual list of operations, as in Figure 8.27. Here, the 'Applicant applies' event has two operations which are stated in a

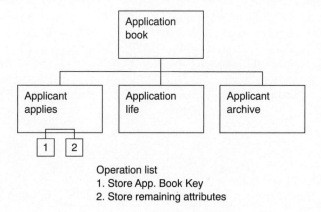

Operation list
1. Store App. Book Key
2. Store remaining attributes

Figure 8.27

separate operations list. Operations are not particularly important at the Analysis phase, but are very useful in Design and Implementation.

8.8 State indicators

State indicators attempt to show the state of the ELH before and after an event. In fact, what they show most clearly are the events that could have happened immediately prior to a given event. Before adding state indicators to an ELH, each event must be given a number. This is usually done numerically starting from 1, left to right, top to bottom, following the structure of the tree, as in Figure 8.28.

Unfortunately, it is not usual to identify the event numbers explicitly on the diagram. The numbers are implicit from their point in the tree. This can make state indicators difficult to follow.

State indicators are added to each event (leaf node) in the tree. This takes the form of two numbers separated by a slash. The first number is the event number that took place immediately before the event, i.e. the state that the ELH was in prior to the event. In fact, this could be a set of numbers, rather than just a single one, if the event could have been preceded by any one of a number of events. A special case of the first number is a dash, indicating that there were no preceding events.

The second number is the number of the event, i.e. the state that the ELH was in after the event. This also has a special case of dash when there are no following events. This is best illustrated by an example.

In Figure 8.29, the first event 'Ordered items not stocked' has no preceding events, so there is a dash to the left of the slash. The 'after state' is 1 (i.e. after

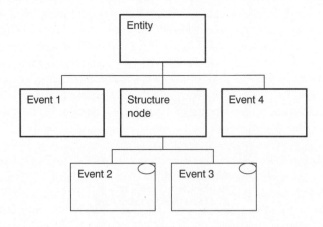

Figure 8.28

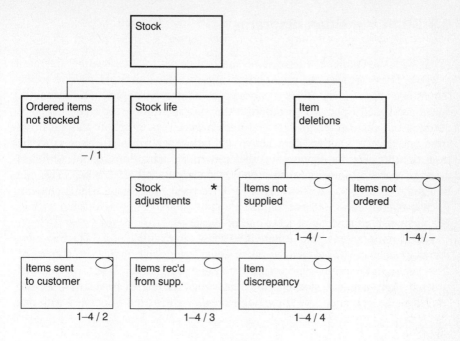

Figure 8.29

event 1), so a 1 goes to the right of the slash. The next event (no. 2) is 'Items sent to customer'. Event 1 will definitely have happened before this event because it is before the structure node for event 2 in a sequence. It could have happened immediately before event 2 if this was the first stock adjustment, so 1 would need to go before the slash. However, there are other possibilities. If event 2 was the first and second stock adjustment, a 2 would also need to go before the slash, i.e. event 2 could have happened immediately before event 2 (there were two in a row). As there is an iteration of stock adjustments, and each could be either event 2, 3 or 4, event 2 could also happen immediately after event 3 or 4. So, event 2 could happen when the ELH is in state 1, 2, 3 or 4. This is written 1–4. The 'after state' is 2, similar to the first event.

Events 3 and 4 are very similar to event 2, but event 5 'Items not supplied' is different. The 'before states' here are again 1–4. It is easy to see that this event could happen immediately after events 2, 3 or 4 because of the sequence at the top level. However, an iteration (stock adjustments) means zero or more occurrences, so event 5 could happen immediately after event 1. Because there is no iteration here, there is no question of event 5 following itself or event 6. At this point in the structure, the selection means that either event 5 or event 6 is carried out (once). As there are no following events the 'after state' is '–'. Similarly for event 6.

8.9 **State transition diagrams**

ELHs with state indicators have some similarities with state transition diagrams (STDs). These are used to provide the time or behavioural perspective in the Yourdon method. Here states are drawn as named rectangles. The names of states are usually phrased to describe the system waiting for some event or carrying out some activity. Arrowed lines between states denote the transition from one state to another. Text above and below a horizontal line next to the transition denotes the condition(s) that caused the transition and the action(s) arising from the transition, respectively. Conditions and actions on STDs can be similar to events and effects that we have been considering in this chapter. Each transition does not have to have a condition and action associated with it, but there will usually be at least one of these.

Let's look at an example. Figure 8.30 shows an example of a STD drawn for the same scenario for which we were considering state indicators above. At first we are in the initial state before the system has started. When we find that ordered items are not stocked (the first event on our ELH earlier), we are moved to the next state 'Awaiting adjustments'. The action associated with this

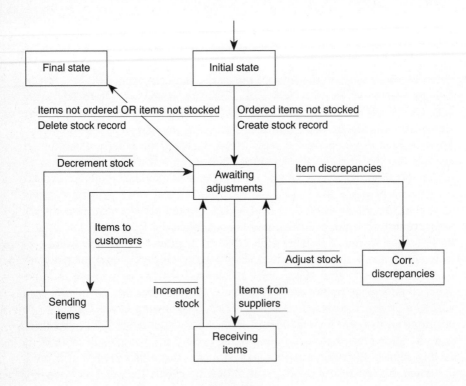

Figure 8.30

transition is 'Create Stock record' (the effect that resulted from the first event on our ELH earlier).

While awaiting adjustments there are three events that might occur: items sent to customers (which causes stock to be decremented), items received from suppliers (which causes stock to be incremented) and item discrepancies (which cause stock adjustments). This is modelled on the STD with intermediate states for sending items, receiving items and correcting discrepancies, together with the appropriate transitions and their attendant conditions and actions. However, the system only stays in these intermediate states long enough to transact its business, before returning to the 'Awaiting adjustments' state.

We eventually get out of the 'Awaiting adjustments' state because items are not ordered or stocked. This transition takes us into the final state with an action to delete the Stock record.

This STD could have been drawn differently. For example, the 'intermediate states' described above could have been missed out, with the three transitions from 'Awaiting adjustments' looping back to itself. However, our aim here was not to examine in any detail how STDs should or could be constructed, but to illustrate the similarities between ELH events and STD conditions, and between DFD effects and STD actions. It was also to illustrate the overall similarity between STDs and ELHs with state indicators.

However, a STD in the Yourdon method would not just be drawn for a single entity in this way. In fact, STDs are usually used as a way of exploding extended real-time DFDs. Yourdon does allow their use for information systems, but this would attempt to model all the events in the system, starting from the context DFD. To manage this, STD explosion is allowed, similar to DFD explosion. So, while there are some similarities between ELHs and STDs, they are likely to be used in quite different ways and result in quite different models in their respective methods.

8.10 Summary

So, what have we learnt about the time-based, behavioural perspective in this chapter? Well, we have learnt about drawing ELHs. We know that we must draw an ELH for each entity on the ERD. Before we start drawing any ELHs, we could draw an entity event matrix. This gives us an event list for each entity, and identifies which events create, modify and delete occurrences of each entity. This helps us to be assured of the completeness of our model.

A good way of identifying events for an entity (whether or not we use an EEM) is to use the DFD. This shows us the effects on the entity and allows us to deduce the events. The event list and the DFD can then be used to construct the ELH, combining the events using the structures of sequence, selection and iteration. Our knowledge of the usual structure of an ELH is also useful in this construction.

We have also looked at some advanced notations for ELHs (parallel structures and quit and resume), but while these are sometimes necessary, they are often best avoided as they complicate the model. We have also seen how operations and state indicators may be added to ELHs.

Finally, we have seen how state transition diagrams may be drawn, and have considered their similarities to ELHs and their likely differences in application.

CHAPTER 9

Structure charts

9.1 Introduction

In previous chapters, we've looked at how a number of techniques can be used to give a complementary model of a system from three perspectives: process, data and behaviour. Most of the techniques correspond to the systems analysis phase of the development life cycle. Also, most of the techniques intend to portray a logical, rather than physical, model of the system. When we were looking at data modelling, we considered how to move the logical model embodied in ERDs on to a more physical model, by either attribution or data normalization. This might be thought of as corresponding more to the systems design phase of the life cycle.

We now need to consider how to move the parts of the logical model towards a physical implementation. In the Yourdon and Gane and Sarson methods, the activity of developing a physical process design from the logical model is known as structured design.

The process parts of the logical model are DFDs and the supporting data dictionary entries. The processes on DFDs are logical and have no physical connotations. That is, they're just things to be done in the system and we don't necessarily expect a one to one correspondence between logical processes and physical programs. This might happen, but equally several processes might join together to make one physical program, or one process might be split to make a number of physical programs.

We document our physical process design on a structure chart. The process by which we partition the logical model into physical units is called transform analysis. Let's look at these one at a time.

9.2 Structure charts

A structure chart shows us the physical units, or modules, that make up a system and what data and control is flowing between them. A module is shown on a structure chart as a named rectangle, as in Figure 9.1.

Notice that the module name is similar to a process name on a DFD: it's an active description of something being done. We can also use pre-defined modules in structure charts, i.e. they already exist in a library somewhere.

```
┌──────────────────────────┐
│ │ Validate Orders      │ │
│ │                      │ │
│ │                      │ │
└──────────────────────────┘
```

Figure 9.1

These are shown as ordinary modules, but with a line down each side. A module might be a program, or it might be a part of a program, like a section or a procedure.

A structure chart is hierarchical, and each module may call and be called by other modules. This is shown by an arrow, called a connection, as in Figure 9.2. Here, the module 'Validate Orders' is the calling module, and 'Read Orders' and 'Read Stock' are the called ones. That is, control initially resides with the calling module. It is then passed to the called module, which does its work, then returns control to the calling module.

Note that we are only defining a calling hierarchy with connections. We are not saying that data is being passed. For example, in Figure 9.2, we are saying only that 'Validate Orders' may call 'Read Orders' and 'Read Stock'. We are not saying that 'Validate Orders' passes data to the two modules. This is modelled using couples that we will come to in a moment.

Note also that there is no implied order in module calls depending on where they appear on the diagram. So, when considering the calls from Validate Orders, it doesn't mean that Read Orders will be called before Read Stock. This means that structure charts don't have a complete notion of sequence. There is some sequence from top to bottom, because calling modules come before called modules. But it doesn't extend beyond that, and we can't tell in which order the called modules will be executed.

The structure chart notation does take account of selection and iteration, though. Selection is shown as a diamond at the root of a number of connections, as in Figure 9.3. Here, only one of these calls will be carried out

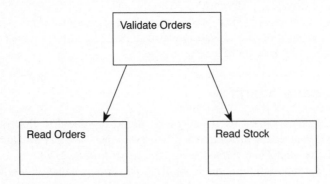

Figure 9.2

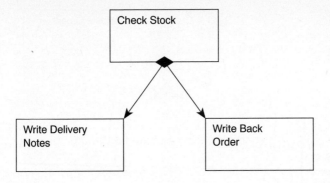

Figure 9.3

for each order when checking stock. If the order is available, 'Write Delivery Notes' will be called. If the order is non-available, 'Write Back Order' will be called.

Iteration is shown as an arrow across the bases of the connections that are repeated, as in Figure 9.4. Here, the calls with the arrow across will be carried out a number of times, while the others will occur only once. So, when the module 'Check Stock' is being executed, the module 'Initialize Variables' will be called only once (presumably at the beginning). 'Validate Orders' and 'Write Delivery Notes' will be called a number of times. And 'Write Order Stats' will be called only once (presumably at the end). However, we'll just stick to the basics here and we won't attempt to model selection and iteration in structure charts again in this chapter.

In general, the calling structure on structure charts is quite free, and modules may call other modules at various levels, several modules may call one module, and so on. However, each structure chart has only one module that is the top of the hierarchy. This is sometimes referred to as the 'boss' module.

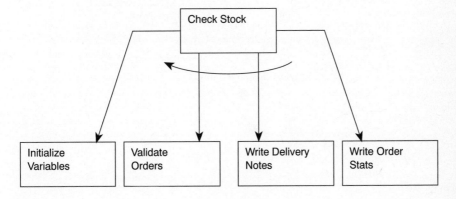

Figure 9.4

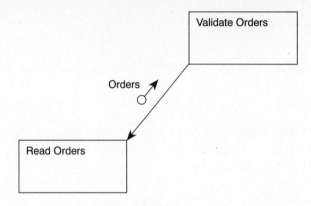

Figure 9.5

Each of the connections on a structure chart may have data and/or control associated with it in one or both directions. These are called couples. Data couples are shown as in Figure 9.5 and denote the passing of data between modules.

There is often confusion between connections and couples. As we saw earlier, a connection does not model the passing of data. So, in Figure 9.5, we are not saying that 'Validate Orders' passes data to 'Read Orders', we are saying that at some point in its execution 'Validate Orders' may call 'Read Orders'. The data passing is shown by the data couple. So, what we are saying about data is that when 'Read Orders' finishes its processing and returns control to 'Validate Orders' it is passing some data 'Orders'.

Control couples are shown as in Figure 9.6 and denote the passing of 'flags' between modules. In this case, when the module 'Validate Orders' has completed its processing and returns control to 'Check Stock' it also returns a flag 'Invalid Order' to say whether the order was valid or not.

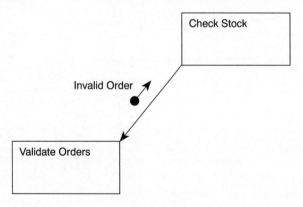

Figure 9.6

9.3 Transform analysis

Those are the conventions for drawing structure charts. Let's see now how they could be derived from DFDs via a process called transform analysis. This is by no means an automatic process and needs a good deal of human intelligence and judgement. However, it does give us some rough rules of thumb by which to proceed.

Obviously the DFD to be used as the starting point for this process should be the required logical DFD. Because the structure chart is going to model the relationship between modules it is only interested in processes that are going to be automated. Also, we want the full set of processes for the required system to be input to this process.

We'll go through the steps of transform analysis one at a time and illustrate them with an example.

EXAMPLE 9.1

Consider the DFD in Figure 9.7. Here, customers send in orders and they're validated against the Stock file. Valid orders are passed on so that stock can be checked. Fully available orders have Delivery Notes printed which are sent to the Warehouse for picking and despatch, and

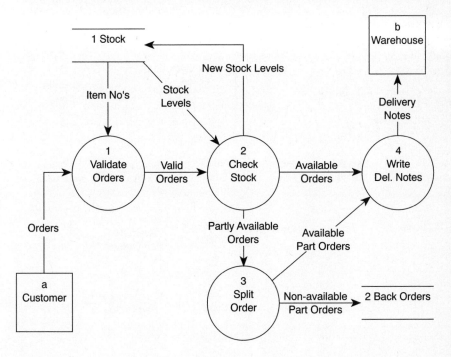

Figure 9.7

stock is updated with new stock levels. Partly available orders are split, with available part orders being treated as fully available orders, and non-available part orders written to the Back Orders file.

First, we'll redraw the DFD removing data stores and external entities, as in Figure 9.8. Now we've made the first movement towards a structure chart. The next step is to identify the central transform of the DFD. That is, we want to find the part of the DFD where all the real work is being done.

To identify the central transform, we want to rule out anything that we'd consider to be purely input or output processing. The simplest way to do this is to look at each process in turn and decide whether it's central or peripheral to the system we're modelling.

Validate Orders could be considered to be input processing. It's checking orders and only passing on those that are valid to the main processing of the system. Write Delivery Notes could be considered to be output processing. It's just formatting and printing output once the main processing of the system has been done. Check Stock could be part of the central transform because it is taking part in the main processing and is after the input has been prepared and before the output is formatted. Split Order could also be considered part of the

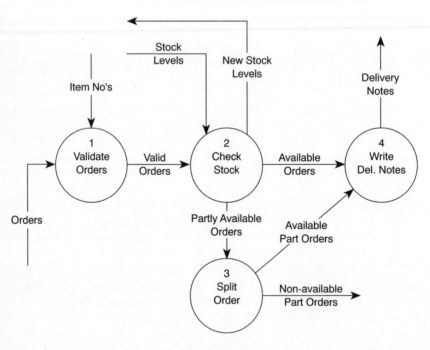

Figure 9.8

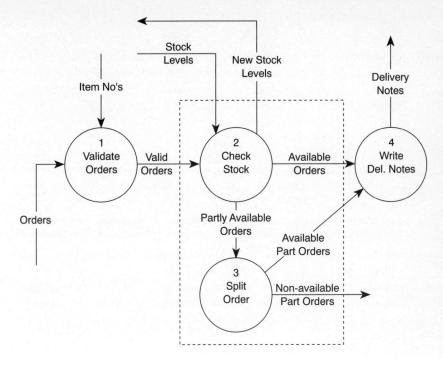

Figure 9.9

central transform for similar reasons. So, we'll mark the central transform as in Figure 9.9.

It's not worth spending hours agonizing over what is and isn't part of the central transform. This isn't an end in itself, it's merely a precursor to the next step, which is to introduce hierarchy. The graphics also point us towards the central transform. Because it is a central transform, we'd expect it to be somewhere in the middle. Also, if we look for the busiest process, or group of processes, we know we're in the right area.

Once we've identified the central transform, the next step is to introduce some hierarchy. The DFD is a free-form diagram, but the structure chart is hierarchical, so we must impose some structure upon the DFD if we are to transform it into a structure chart.

The first step in this process is to select a boss module, that is, a module that will be top of the hierarchy. There are two options here, either choose one of the modules in the central transform, or create a new boss module that calls these modules. The choice depends to some extent on how equal the modules are in the central transform. If one is dominant, it should probably be the boss. If they're all on about the same level, it's probably better to create a new boss module.

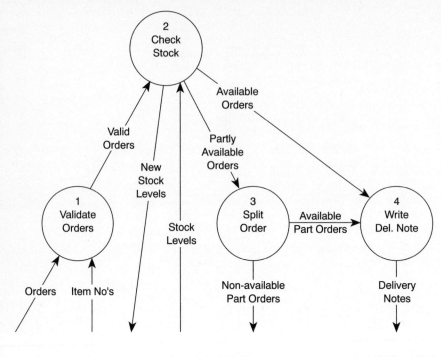

Figure 9.10

There are few alternatives here anyway, so we should try them all out and see what feels best.

In our example, Check Stock is the dominant module in the central transform because it deals with all orders and the other module deals only with some. If we make this the boss module, this would give us a start to our structure chart as in Figure 9.10.

Notice that the diagram is syntactically the same as before, it is just drawn differently to give the impression of hierarchy. That is, this is just the stripped DFD rearranged with the boss module at the top.

The other alternative is to create a new boss module. This would give us a start to our structure chart as in Figure 9.11, with a new boss module 'Process Orders' in charge of the two modules from the central transform.

Notice that the modules in the central transform no longer communicate directly, and do so via the new boss module. This works well, and there's always an attraction in having a new boss module in charge that's dedicated to calling and communicating with other modules, without the distraction of its own work. However, in this case it feels right for Split Order to be subordinate to Check Stock, so we'll continue with our first alternative.

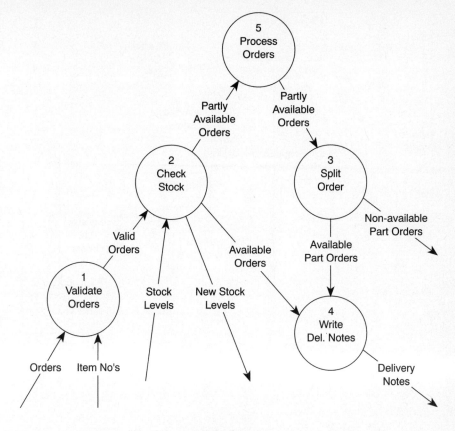

Figure 9.11

Once this has been decided, we can redraw the diagram so it looks more like a structure chart. There are a number of things that need to be done here. First, the modules can be drawn as rectangles rather than as process shapes. Second, the data flows should be replaced by connections with data couples moving in the appropriate direction (see Figure 9.12).

Redrawing the modules as rectangles is simple, but the connections and couples need more care. The difference between connections and couples has been emphasized, but we can see now how a DFD helps us to develop that part of the structure chart notation. For example, in the DFD in Figure 9.10 there is a data flow from 'Validate Orders' to 'Check Stock'. In the structure chart in Figure 9.12, there is now a connection in the opposite direction (to say that 'Check Stock' calls 'Validate Orders'), and a data couple in the direction of the original data flow. In general, structure charts should be drawn with the connections pointing down the hierarchy. The data couples will point

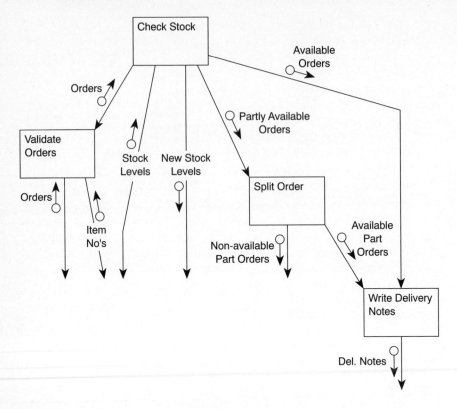

Figure 9.12

in the direction of the original data flows. This can be confirmed by checking the data flows in Figure 9.10 against the data couples in Figure 9.12.

Most of the couples on a structure chart will be data couples, but control couples should be added where necessary. They are often needed after checking or validation. For example, in Figure 9.13, we could add a control couple Valid Order that is returned after the module Validate Orders has completed. Also, if there is a batch or stream of input driving the system, a control couple may be needed to say that this has finished. For example, Orders could be considered to be such a stream, so we could add a control couple End of Orders to be returned when the orders have all been read, as in Figure 9.13.

At this point, we have progressed some way into the physical implementation, with control flags identified and decisions made about batch and transaction processing. In Figure 9.13, the End of Orders control couple was introduced to control the batch processing of orders. If orders were to be processed by the system one at a time by transaction processing no such flag would be necessary.

Finally, we need to tidy up the loose ends. This generally means adding read and write modules. In this example there are several loose ends resulting from the deletion of stores and externals. In most cases, we just need to add a module with a name describing what is being read or written as in Figure 9.14.

For example, the 'loose end' at the bottom-left corner of Figure 9.13 with an incoming stream of orders has been completed in Figure 9.14 with a module 'Read Orders'. The other loose ends in Figure 9.13 can be matched against the read/write modules in Figure 9.14 similarly. The read/write modules have now filled the gap where the stores and externals on the original DFD were deleted. It is no surprise, therefore, that if we look back at the original DFD (Figure 9.7) the read/write modules on the structure chart correspond to the stores and the data flows from and to the externals.

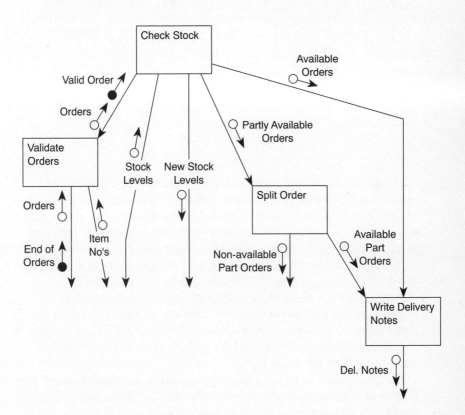

Figure 9.13

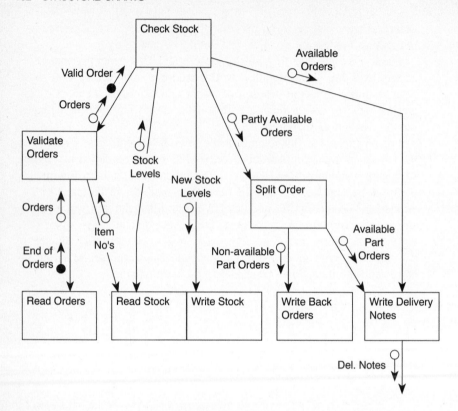

Figure 9.14

Sometimes it doesn't really make sense to add a module and the connection is deleted. For example, there's no point in adding another module called Write Delivery Note to the remaining loose end at the bottom-right of Figure 9.14, so we'll delete the connection. This then gives us a first-cut structure chart as in Figure 9.15.

The final step in the transform analysis process is to revise the first-cut structure chart, if this is necessary. There is a good deal of common sense involved in this, although structured design does promote the notions of coupling and cohesion to help us to think about some of the issues. Several types of both coupling and cohesion may be identified, and these may be ranked from best to worst, but we'll just define the terms here.

Coupling looks at the type of communication between modules. We want low coupling between modules so that they are as independent (or loosely coupled) as possible to give us maximum flexibility and ability to change. Cohesion looks at how the activities within each

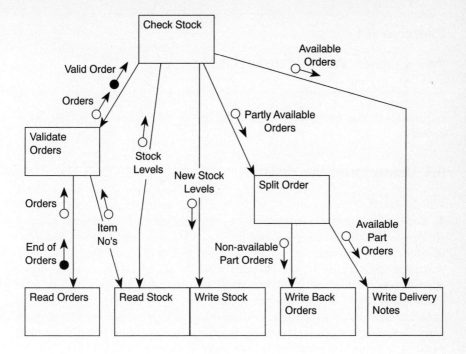

Figure 9.15

module are related. We want modules that are highly cohesive, where each module carries out a single, definable function.

Remembering these principles, while we might expect modules on a structure chart to be called from more than one place, if this is happening with different inputs or outputs there might be a problem with the cohesion of the module. Looking back to Figure 9.15, 'Write Delivery Notes' is called from 'Check Stock' with a data couple 'Available Orders', and from 'Split Order' with a data couple 'Available Part Orders'. In this case it's probably safe to assume that 'Available Orders' and 'Available Part Orders' are equivalent and that there is no problem.

It's obvious that the module Read Stock is doing two separate things, though. It's getting item numbers for one module and getting stock levels for another module. We could split the module, but it probably isn't really necessary in this case because both pieces of data come from the same data store, so we'll leave it as it is. It might lead us to question whether 'Read Stock' needs to be passed a control couple so that it knows whether to return item numbers or stock levels.

Exercise 9.1

Draw a structure chart from the DFD in Figure 9.16.

A solution to this exercise is walked through in the Appendix, starting on p. 225.

9.4 Using structure charts

We can see from the example and exercise how useful structure charts can be in thinking about the structure of a program and its parameter passing. However, structured design has not been popular, even among those that have adopted structured analysis. One reason for this is the way that it has been promoted: as a means of transforming a whole set of DFDs into a structure chart. We've been working on only small examples, but imagine how difficult transform analysis would be with a large set of DFDs. Also, the resulting structure chart could supposedly contain a hierarchy of programs and program parts. This might work for some types of system. You could imagine a large piece of systems software like an operating system, or a CASE tool, being a large hierarchy of modules acting in a coordinated way. However, for many information systems this is absurd. In these systems there might be a mix of sub-systems that operate in different ways on different timescales. For example, parts of the system might be online transaction processing, while other parts might be weekly and monthly batch runs. In this situation, a single hierarchy of modules will clearly not work.

However, on the level that we have been looking at it, transform analysis and structure charts are clearly useful. The answer is to partition the set of DFDs into physical units before applying these techniques. So, for each physical unit, a separate structure chart would be drawn. This allows transform analysis and structure charts to be applied where they are useful – at the sub-program level as a way of thinking about program structure and parameter passing between the parts.

9.5 Summary

In this chapter we've seen how to advance the logical process perspective from the systems analysis phase towards a physical process design in the systems design phase. When we remember that we already have the contents of each of the modules specified quite tightly in Structured English, or something similar, in the data dictionary, it is clear that we are getting quite close to coding. In fact, this is as far as structured systems analysis

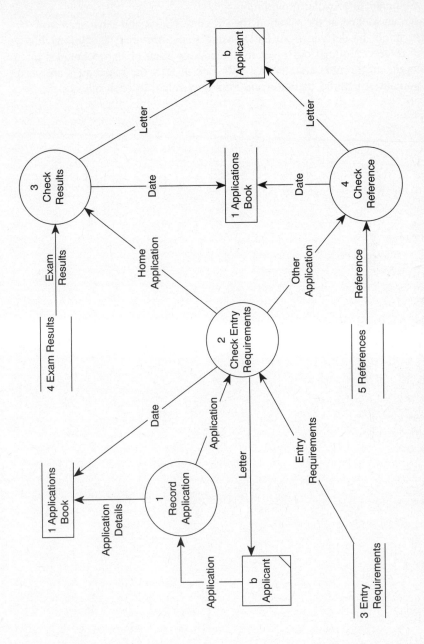

Figure 9.16

and structured design takes us before we get on to the next phase of the development life cycle: programming.

We've looked at the notation for structure charts and have seen how these might be derived from DFDs using transform analysis. Before this we have largely confined ourselves to considering each of the techniques in isolation. In the next chapter, we will look at how the techniques are used in popular structured methods and how they relate to each other.

CHAPTER 10

Structured methods

10.1 Introduction

Apart from the first chapter, this book has concentrated almost exclusively on structured techniques, i.e. DFDs, ERDs etc. But any single technique cannot stand alone and must be combined with other techniques to form a coherent way of modelling an information system. Such a set of structured techniques is generally referred to as a structured method (or, unhappily, a structured methodology, or even, cynically, a 'structured mythology').

Methods have been referred to in passing in looking at techniques, mostly to point out that some have differences in notation in different methods. In this chapter, the focus is on the methods themselves. We will be concentrating on the SSADM and Yourdon methods. In each case we will consider the structure, or life cycle, of the method and where the various techniques fit into it. We will also consider how techniques develop as the method goes through succeeding phases and how the different techniques should correspond to each other to promote consistency and completeness. Finally, the methods will be compared and analysed, and a possible convergence discussed.

10.2 SSADM

SSADM covers the early phases of the systems development life cycle, concentrating on feasibility study and systems analysis, with some coverage of systems design. Within this part of the life cycle, the method is organized into seven stages within five modules, as in Figure 10.1

The modules represent phases, or sub-phases, of the part of the life cycle that we are interested in. It is clear that the Feasibility module corresponds to the Feasibility Study phase, that the Requirements Analysis and Requirements Specification modules correspond to the Systems Analysis phase, and that the Physical Design module corresponds to the Systems Design phase. The Logical System Specification phase has elements of both Systems Analysis and Systems Design.

The stages define the activities that must be carried out to apply the method. Each stage is broken down into a number of steps that detail the tasks to be carried out. Also, the deliverables are defined, in terms of both intermediate and end products. We do not need to go into this level of detail here because our purpose is merely to map the techniques onto this 'structural model' (as it is known in SSADM).

Data flow diagrams are first used in SSADM in the Feasibility module, where a Context Diagram and Current Physical DFD are developed. These are then developed further in the Requirements Analysis module. In Investigation of the Current Environment, the DFD is exploded and 'logicalized' to produce a logical DFD. In Business System Options, the final transformation towards a required DFD begins. Here, a top-level required DFD is prepared for each of the options. When one of these is selected, a full, exploded required DFD is prepared in the Requirements Specification module.

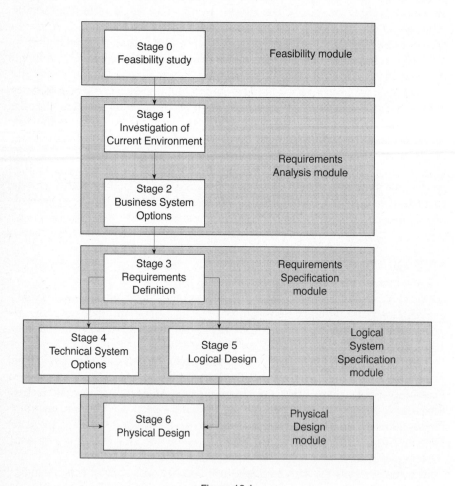

Figure 10.1

SSADM does not have a data dictionary exactly as we studied it in Chapters 5 and 6, but it does have a dictionary. This records information about all the elements of all the techniques used in the method, be they graphical or textual. In this way, the SSADM dictionary pervades all stages of the method. The parts of the SSADM dictionary that correspond most closely with a data dictionary are Function Definitions, I–O Descriptions and I–O structures. These evolve through the Requirements Analysis and Requirements Specification modules. They are created in Investigation of the Current Environment, to define the functions, inputs and outputs of the current system. These are then developed in Requirements Definition, to address the functions, inputs and outputs of the required system.

Data modelling is carried out in SSADM using both ERDs and normalization. The terminology is different in both cases, though. ERDs are drawn using the crow's feet notation and are called logical data structure (LDS) diagrams. These form the logical data model (LDM), together with entity and relationship descriptions. Normalization is called relational data analysis (RDA).

An overview LDS diagram is first drawn in the Feasibility module. This is developed into a current LDM in Investigation of the Current Environment. In Stage 2, an LDM for each Business System Option is produced. When a Business System Option is selected, the appropriate LDM is developed further in the Requirements Specification module to arrive at the Required Data Model. RDA (normalization) is then applied to this to produce the Required System LDM.

ELHs are used after many of the other techniques and do not put in an appearance until the end of the Requirements Specification module. Here, an entity event matrix (EEM) is produced, and ELHs are developed for each entity. Operations are included at this stage, but state indicators are not added until Stage 5, Logical Design.

There are many other techniques that are used in the various steps and stages of SSADM, but it is beyond the scope of the book to go into all of them here. We do want to pursue how the essential techniques that we have studied relate to each other in SSADM, though. In all cases here we are talking about the final model that emerges, as most techniques go through an evolution of different stages.

The relationship between DFDs and ERDs centres on data stores and entities, respectively. Each data store on the DFD must correspond to one or more entities on the ERD, but each entity on the ERD must correspond only to one data store on the DFD. The rationale for this is that the ERD should be the place where the detailed data modelling is done, but to reflect all of this on the DFD would overwhelm it with data when it is primarily concerned with process.

The relationship between ERDs and ELHs is simple. For each entity on the ERD there should be an ELH. The relationship between DFDs and ELHs is informal and more complicated. As we saw in Chapter 8, we can see effects on data stores on the DFD (which we can trace back to entities on the ERD), which will allow us to deduce the events that caused the effects. The events can then be entered into the EEM and form the basis for drawing ELHs. So, events (leaf nodes) on ELHs should correspond to effects (data store updates) on DFDs.

The relationship between the SSADM dictionary and the other techniques is simple. All the elements of the techniques (e.g. stores on DFDs, relationships on ERDs) have an entry in the dictionary.

10.3 The Yourdon method

Like SSADM, the Yourdon method concentrates on the early phases of the development life cycle: Feasibility Study, Systems Analysis and Systems Design. These phases are called Survey, Systems Analysis, and Design, respectively, in Yourdon.

In the Survey phase, the only structured technique that is used is data flow diagramming in preparing a context diagram. This goes into the Project Charter, together with details of responsible users, current problems, goals and objectives, and technical and economic feasibility. The Project Charter is then presented for a management decision.

If the project continues, it progresses to the Systems Analysis phase. In this phase and the next (Design) the emphasis is on using the structured techniques to build a series of models, as in Figure 10.2.

The first of these, the Implementation Model, is the only one that is optional. It should be avoided if possible, but can be used to model the current system (i.e. the current implementation). Yourdon's view is that analysts spend too much time modelling the current system because it is obvious how to do that (go and ask the people that are running it now). This might lead to the analyst getting bogged down in all the detail, much of which might not be needed for the new system. Therefore, Yourdon's advice is to go straight for the Essential Model. This is a model that captures the essence of the new system, what we might think of as a required logical model.

However, Yourdon does allow that the Implementation Model might be needed sometimes, and in my experience it would be very difficult to start addressing the requirements of a new system without modelling the operation of the current system, at least in some rudimentary way. The Implementation Model is not very detailed in any case, probably only containing a top-level DFD and an ERD. It might also contain a few process specifications and some physical documents that have been collected, but that is all.

The first model proper in the Yourdon method is the Essential Model. This consists of an Environmental and a Behavioural Model. The aim of the

SURVEY

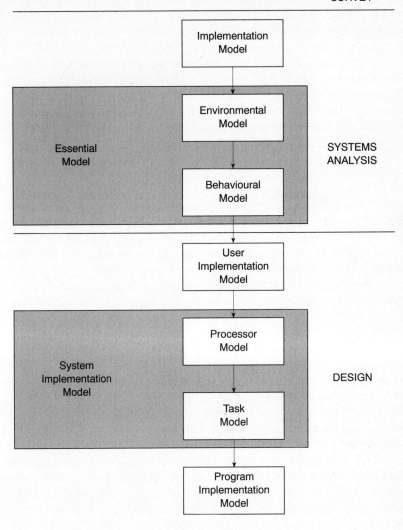

Figure 10.2

Environmental Model is to define the environment, or context, of the system. This contains

- A context diagram
- An event list
- A statement of purpose.

The context diagram is a development of the one produced in the Survey. It should be consistent with the event list in that all the events in the list should be visible on the context diagram in some way. The statement of purpose is just a short textual statement of the purpose of the system. Although not compulsory, the Environmental Model could also contain an initial data dictionary and ERD.

The Behavioural Model defines the behaviour of the system. It is here that most of the techniques that we have studied are developed to the full. A levelled set of required logical DFDs is produced by event partitioning. Also, a complete ERD (using the diamond notation) and data dictionary are developed, the latter including full data descriptions and process specifications. All parts of the Behavioural Model are cross-checked.

The main result of the Systems Analysis phase, the Essential Model, is then passed into the Design phase. The first model here is the User Implementation Model. This addresses how the system will be implemented from the user's point of view and contains a Human Interface specification and any operational constraints. It uses state transition diagrams to define user/system dialogues. It also updates the Essential Model by adding an automation boundary to the ERD and DFD. This leads to the sort of changes to the DFD that we studied in Chapter 3 when considering the movement from current logical to required logical model. The updated Essential Model is then rechecked.

The Systems Implementation Model addresses how the system will be implemented from the developer's point of view. The DFD from the User Implementation Model provides the main input. This is used to develop first a Processor Model and then a Task Model. The Processor Model is only needed if the system is to be run across several different processors (i.e. computers). If it is developed, different processes and stores from the DFD are allocated to different processors and the inter-processor communication is defined. That is, the model of the system in the form of the DFD is partitioned across the different computers that will be used to run the system.

This is then taken further in the Task Model when processes and stores from the DFD are assigned to separate tasks, i.e. separate programs or parts of programs. It is completed in the Program Implementation Model when a structure chart is developed for each task in the Task Model using transform analysis. The structure charts are then evaluated using coupling and cohesion.

The consistency and completeness checks in Yourdon are simple one to one existence checks. For the most part these are unremarkable, e.g. there is no doubt that it is sensible to expect data descriptions in the data dictionary for each store and flow, and a process specification for each process that is a functional primitive. The only controversial check is between the DFD and ERD. Here the rule is that each store on the DFD should correspond to one entity or relationship on the ERD. As we saw in Chapter 7, it can be argued that this is too simplistic and certainly SSADM takes a different view.

10.4 Method comparison and evaluation

This leads us neatly into a broad comparison and evaluation of the two methods and, indeed, of structured methods altogether. It can be seen that the two methods use a broadly similar set of structured techniques embedded in their own life cycle. Both use DFDs in similar ways, although their development is quite different. There is less emphasis on modelling the current system in Yourdon, and the diagrams are developed by event partitioning rather than top-down as in SSADM. Both methods use ERDs, but here there is less similarity because they use different notations (the diamond notation in Yourdon and the crow's feet notation in SSADM). Also, normalization plays an important part in SSADM, but not in Yourdon. Both methods have a dictionary of some sort, but here again there is a significant difference. SSADM uses ELHs to model the behavioural perspective and there is really no corresponding technique for this in Yourdon. Conversely, Yourdon uses structure charts to model the implementation of a program and there is no corresponding technique for this in SSADM.

The various stages and steps of SSADM, and the various models of Yourdon, can be overwhelming at first, and structured methods have been criticized for being too bureaucratic. Certainly, SSADM in particular has often been seen as a sledgehammer to crack a nut, with its bewildering array of ancillary techniques to complement the structured techniques, in addition to all the terminology and rigidity of the 'structural model'. Yourdon is not as bad in these respects, but it lacks the strong behavioural perspective of SSADM to complement the process and data perspectives. Nor is it as convincing in the balancing of the three views in terms of consistency and completeness.

10.5 The Griffiths methodology?

While the methods have some detractors, these criticisms do not concern the essential structured techniques that we have studied in this book. In fact we have discussed the application of the techniques as we have gone along and my own way of applying them is as follows.

At the Feasibility Study phase, a top-level current logical DFD should be drawn (as we saw in Chapter 2) to help understanding of the system. If the new system is likely to be significantly different, then it is also worth drawing a top-level required logical model (as we saw in Chapter 3) to help in thinking about the likely costs and benefits in moving from one to the other. The models in themselves are not important at this stage, they are just ways of thinking about the system and change.

At the Systems Analysis phase, a full set of DFDs should be prepared. These should be exploded required logical DFDs (as we saw in Chapters 2–4). A full data dictionary should be developed including data descriptions and process specifications (Chapters 5 and 6). An ERD should be developed using the crow's feet notation (Chapter 7) and an ELH should be developed for each entity (Chapter 8).

At the Systems Design phase, entities should be normalized (Chapter 8). Also, Processor and Task Models should be prepared and Structure Charts developed for each task (Chapter 9).

Consistency and completeness checks should be carried out between all techniques and models as appropriate. All the objects on the DFD set (i.e. all processes, flows, stores and externals) should be described in the data dictionary. The data parts should be described in terms of data elements and data structures. The stores on the DFD should correspond to one or more entities on the ERD. The effects on the DFDs should correspond to the events on the ELHs. The DFDs should be partitioned in the Processor and Task Models and should be traceable to the modules and connections on the structure charts.

Entities and relationships should be described in the data dictionary. Each entity should be described by an ELH. Each entity should be normalized.

10.6 Structured techniques

Structured techniques have come a long way since their inception in the mid-1970s when there really were no techniques at all for carrying out systems analysis. They have been tried and tested, and have evolved, in intensive usage in industry by thousands of systems analysts. Other types of method still have this road to travel. Structured techniques represent the most mature, balanced and reliable way that we have today to model information systems.

Solutions to exercises

Exercise 2.1

When a request is received from a customer, the sales office raises an order. Orders are passed to the credit control department where the customer's credit worthiness is checked. If credit approval is not granted, the order is referred back to the sales office for the attention of the sales manager. If the order is accepted, it is passed to the stock office where the availability of each item on the order is checked by the stock clerk. If all the items on the order are available in full, the order is passed to the warehouse for picking and despatch and the stock clerk adjusts the stock cards accordingly. If the order cannot be completely satisfied out of current stock the stock clerk will split the order. The clerk will raise a part-order out of those items and quantities which **can** be met from current stock and this is passed to the warehouse, the stock-cards being adjusted accordingly. The balance of the customer's order is used to raise another part-order which the stock clerk places in a 'back-orders file'.

If while adjusting a stock-card, the stock clerk observes that the stock level of an item now falls below the stipulated reorder level, the stock clerk must inform the purchasing department which is now responsible for replenishing the stock.

Draw a DFD to model this system.

SOLUTION

In this solution, we'll go through the problem statement step by step and build up a DFD. Don't worry if your solution isn't the same as this, as there are many correct models of an information system. However, there are some things that you may have done wrong, so we'll talk about these as we go through.

So, the first sentence of the problem statement tells us 'When a request is received from a customer, the sales office raises an order.' From this we get the main input, 'Request', the source, 'Customer',

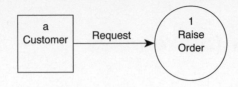

Figure A.1

and the process, 'Raise Order'. This gives us a start to our DFD as in Figure A.1. Note that the subject, the sales office, doesn't appear on the diagram.

In the second sentence 'Orders are passed to the credit control department where the customer's credit worthiness is checked'. From this we get the data flow, 'Order', and the process that's carried out on this flow, 'Check Credit'. This builds on to our DFD as in Figure A.2. Notice again that the subject, the credit control department, does not appear on the diagram.

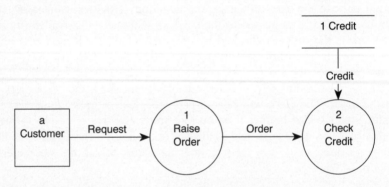

Figure A.2

It would be reasonable to invent a data store of credit details at this point, to allow the checking of credit. See how the flow direction is into the process, showing that the data store is being read.

In the next sentence 'If credit approval is not granted, the order is referred back to the sales office for the attention of the sales manager'. From this we find a flow, 'Rejected Order', and its destination, 'the Sales Manager' (or 'Sales Office'). At this point, we have no alternative but to represent this on our diagram as in Figure A.3.

The sales manager is shown as an external here because, while the person is carrying out a process inside the system, we have no information about that process. The sales manager is just a black hole where orders which fail the credit check are sent. In a real situation,

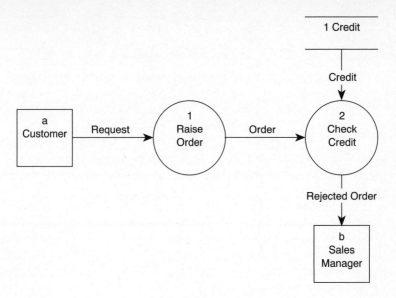

Figure A.3

this would prompt the analyst to investigate what the sales manager did with those orders so that this could be drawn on the diagram.

Notice that the name chosen for the flow is more precise than just 'Order'. In general, names on the diagram should be chosen carefully, to convey as much meaning as possible in the small amount of space available.

In the next sentence 'If the order is accepted, it is passed to the stock office where the availability of each item on the order is checked by the stock clerk'. From this we find a flow, 'Accepted Order', and the process that operates upon it, 'Check Availability'. This might be drawn on the diagram as in Figure A.4. As in the second process, a data store might be invented to provide information for the checking.

In the next sentence 'If all the items on the order are available in full, the order is passed to the warehouse for picking and despatch and the stock clerk adjusts the stock cards accordingly'. From this we find a flow, 'Fully Available Order', and possibly two processes, 'adjust stock' and 'pass orders'. The first process could be drawn as in Figure A.5.

Notice the two-way flow that's introduced here. This is because the data is first read by the process, then the stock cards are updated within the process, then the adjusted cards are written back to the store. The second process 'passing orders to the warehouse' is fairly trivial and while we could show it explicitly on the diagram, there is

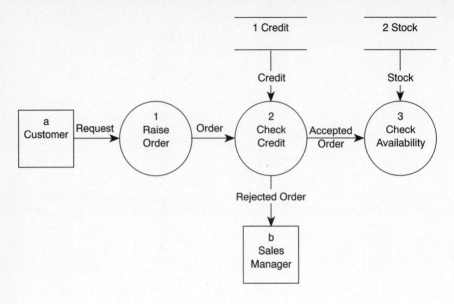

Figure A.4

really no need. We can think of the actual process as going on inside 'Adjust Stock'.

Note that we're not interested in the actual picking of goods at the warehouse or their despatch to customers, because this is material flow rather than data flow. In this case the warehouse is a valid external entity because we see it as the destination for some data ('Order Details') that we're sending out of the system. It's only if our brief included the computerization of the warehouse itself that we would want to investigate the picking and despatch procedures, and draw these on the diagram.

In the next sentence 'If the order cannot be completely satisfied out of current stock, the stock clerk will split the order'. From this we get a process, 'split order', and an implied flow of Partly Available Orders. This might be drawn on the diagram as in Figure A.6.

In the next sentence 'The clerk will raise a part order out of those items and quantities which **can** be met from current stock, and this is passed to the warehouse, the stock cards being adjusted accordingly'. This is exactly the same as for Fully Available Orders and may use the same process by linking directly to it, as in Figure A.7. In this case the name of the flow needs to be chosen carefully so that it's clear exactly what's happening on the diagram.

The next sentence tells us 'The balance of the customer's order is used to raise another part order which the stock clerk places in a back orders file'. Here we have a flow, Part Order; a store, Back Orders;

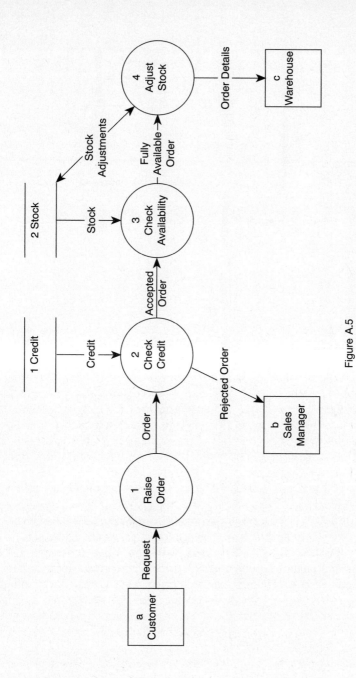

Figure A.5

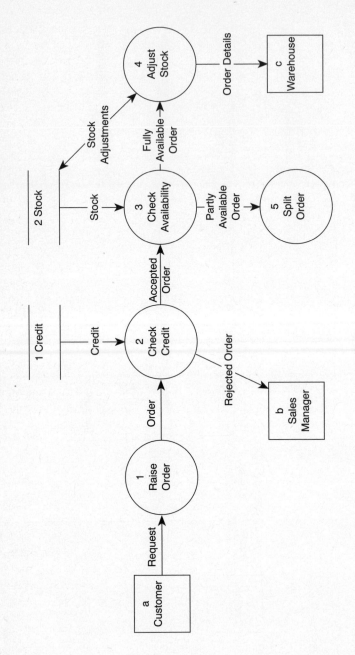

Figure A.6

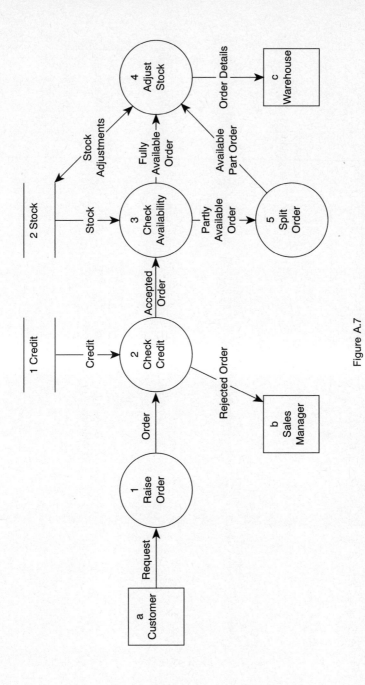

Figure A.7

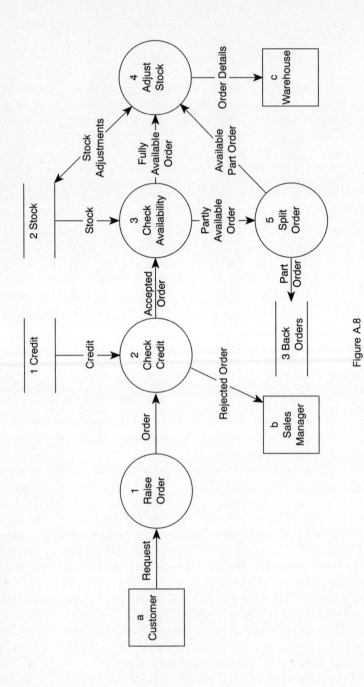

Figure A.8

and the process that sends the flow to the store. Again the process is trivial and we might consider it to be going on inside 'Split Order'. This gives us an extension to our diagram as in Figure A.8.

The next sentence says 'If while adjusting a stock-card, the stock clerk observes that the stock level of an item now falls below the stipulated reorder level, the stock clerk must inform the purchasing department, which is now responsible for replenishing the stock'. The observation that stock is low is not a process in itself, merely something that's noticed while another process is being carried out (adjusting stock). Informing Purchasing is a process, but is similar to some of the other 'Output' processes that we've not shown explicitly on the diagram. Therefore, we might extend the diagram as in Figure A.9.

The purchasing department is a valid external entity similar to the warehouse. It's just a destination for our requisition notes and we have no information about what actually happens to them. It's only if we wanted to computerize the purchasing department that we'd investigate further and try to draw their procedures on the diagram.

Exercise 3.1

An oil company has two road distribution terminals on Teesside – one at North Tees and one at South Bank. All 'office work' is carried out at the North Tees site.

Orders are received from customers by telephone and noted on a despatch note (DN). These details are extended from a customer card index and filed by requested delivery date.

The day before despatch, orders are routed. The South Bank terminal is advised by telephone of orders to be despatched from there the following day. At North Tees, DNs are passed to the despatch clerk who places them in pigeonholes by vehicle. The next day these are given to drivers when they arrive. The drivers stamp the DN at the pump when loading to show the quantity loaded. They then deliver the product and obtain a signature on the DN from the recipient. The day after delivery, South Bank telephones the North Tees office to advise details of quantities delivered. At North Tees, the despatch clerk receives the previous day's DNs from the drivers as they arrive and passes them to the office.

In the office, DN details for customers in the private sector are entered at a PC. These are then transmitted to head office where invoices are produced and sent to customers. All aspects of payment are dealt with at head office.

For public sector customers, North Tees maintains records of quantities delivered and sends out invoices at month-end. Note that the company

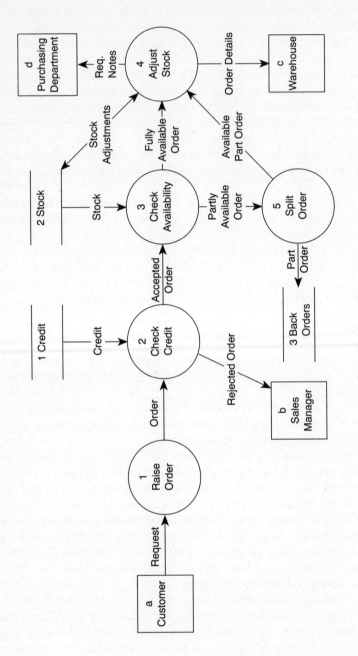

Figure A.9

despatches a number of different products, each with a different selling price. Again, all aspects of payment are dealt with by head office.

Duty is paid to Customs and Excise at the end of each month by North Tees for product delivered to both public and private sector customers. To this end, details of totals delivered by product are maintained (for both terminals). At month-end, a cheque is sent to Customs together with a statement giving the breakdown by product. Duty is levied at different rates for different products.

A current logical DFD of this system, with automation boundary marked, is presented as Figure A.10.

One problem with the system is names and addresses being out of date on invoices for public sector customers. This is because the information is put onto the delivery note at the time of the original order and by the time delivery has been made and an invoice raised, two months could have passed. This makes for delays in payment which management are obviously unhappy about.

A new requirement from head office is that they want to receive a monthly summary by product of the amount invoiced (for public sector customers) and the amount paid in duty (for all customers).

Draw a required logical DFD to model the new system.

SOLUTION

In Exercise 3.1, the processes to be automated have already been chosen, so we just have to concentrate on redrawing the DFD.

The first point to consider is how to redraw the part of the diagram outside the development area. There are five flows that cross the automation boundary. Three are connected directly to an external entity, so we don't need to touch these.

There's a flow 'private sector delivery note' that crosses the boundary and goes first to a process 'Enter Delivery Note Details', and then on to an external 'Head Office'. Here we can simply remove the process from the diagram.

There is another flow 'Delivery Note' that crosses the boundary coming in from the process 'Deliver Orders'. Here we want to remove the process and anything else that's upstream. We can't have the flow coming in from nowhere, so we replace this leg of the diagram with an external entity, say 'Despatch Clerk'.

At this point, we could merge the two externals 'South Bank' and 'Despatch Clerk', because they both generate a flow of delivery details into the system. These changes would result in a DFD as in Figure A.11.

The next thing to consider is how to redraw the part of the diagram inside the automation boundary. If we look first at the data input, the

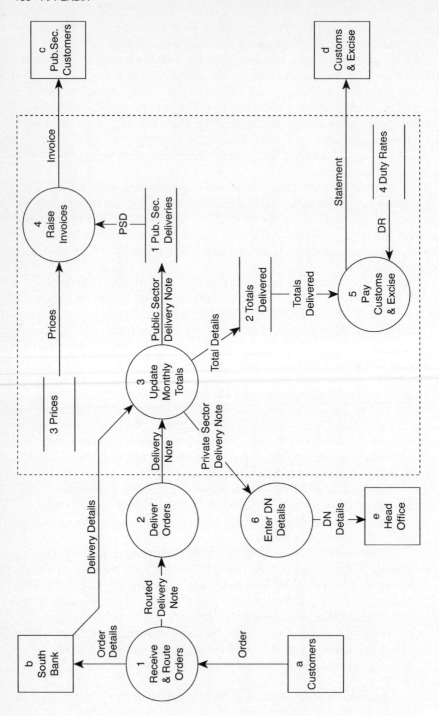

Figure A.10

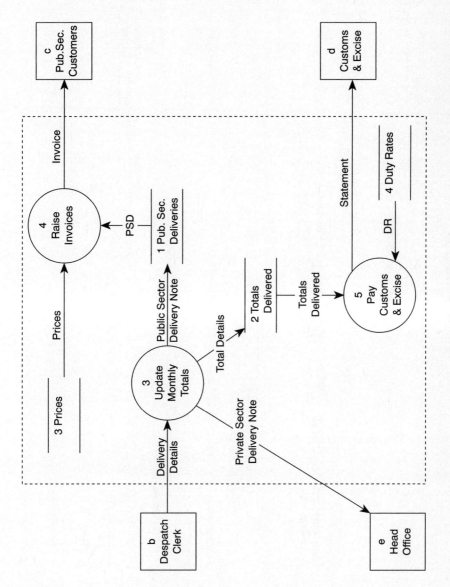

Figure A.11

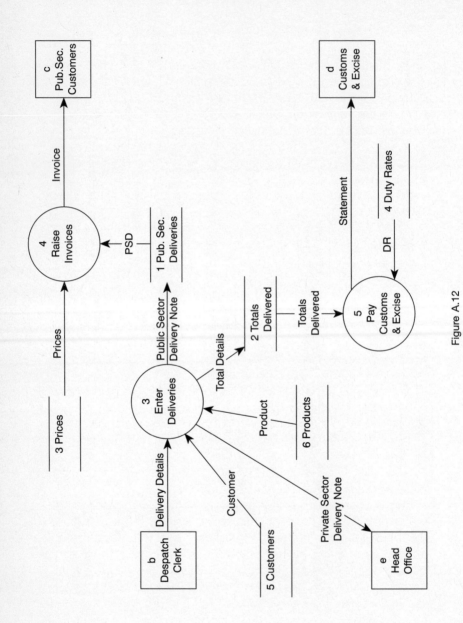

Figure A.12

process 'Update Monthly Totals' is the point where this takes place. A better description for this in a computerized system might be 'Enter Deliveries'.

We also need to consider the provision of data stores to help data validation. It would be reasonable to expect that delivery details included customer and product identification. Therefore, we could add stores to the diagram to allow verification that these had been entered correctly (see Figure A.12).

If we now look at the data stores, we can see that some are logically similar. It was stated that 'duty rates' and 'prices' were held by product, so we could merge these two stores together to make 'products'. This would be a store where we held a duty rate and price for each product. It could be the same 'products' store that's used for validation. So, three stores on our diagram might be combined, as in Figure A.13.

There is also a case for combining 'Public Sector Deliveries' and 'Totals Delivered' because both are recording deliveries. We could merge these two stores to form a new store 'Deliveries'. It's important to note that we're only concerned at this point with how the stores might go together logically and we're saying nothing about what the eventual physical structure might be.

The last point that we need to consider about data stores is their maintenance. The 'Deliveries' store is OK because it is both read from and written to. However, the other two are only read and need update processes to allow them to be changed.

We could imagine that changes in customer details would come from customers. The 'Products' data store might get changes from two places. Price changes could come from head office and duty rate changes from Customs and Excise. This would result in a diagram as in Figure A.14.

Now that we've looked at data input and data stores, we need to consider the problems and new requirements.

One problem that was identified was the names and addresses being out of date on invoices for public sector customers. This was because the information was put on to the delivery note at the time of the original order and by the time delivery had been made and an invoice raised, two months could have passed. This made for delays in payment which management were obviously unhappy about.

A solution to this problem would be to put just a customer number on the original delivery note and then pick up the name and address from the up-to-date 'Customer' store when the invoice is being raised. To do this, all we need is a flow of 'Customer Details' from the 'Customer' store to the 'Raise Invoice' process (see Figure A.15).

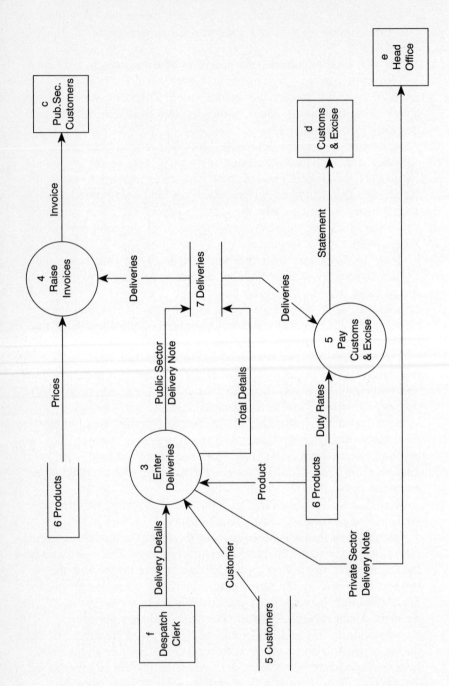

Figure A.13

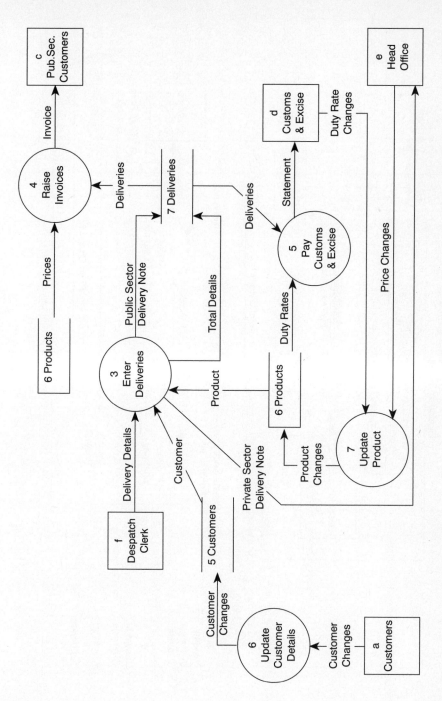

Figure A.14

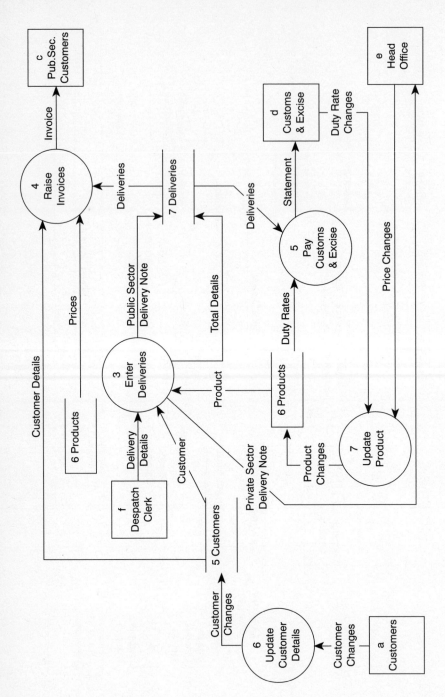

Figure A.15

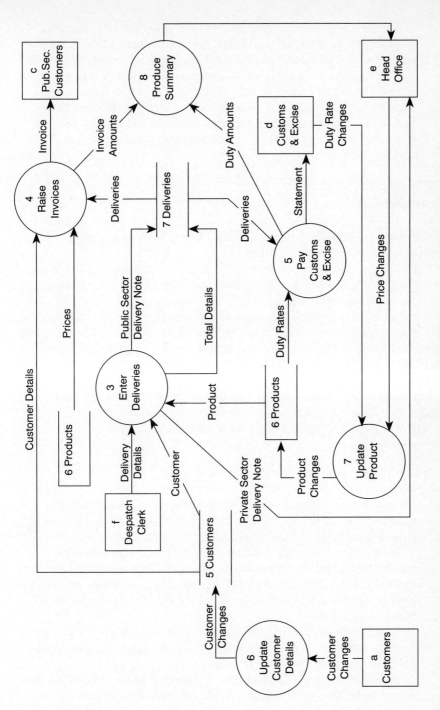

Figure A.16

The new requirement identified was the provision of a monthly summary by product for head office, giving the amount invoiced (for public sector customers) and the total amount paid in duty. To do this we need a new process 'Produce Summary', and a flow going to head office. The inputs to this process would be the public sector invoice amounts and the total duty amounts. These could come from the 'Raise Invoices' process and the 'Pay Customs and Excise' process respectively (see Figure A.16 on the previous page).

Exercise 4.1

In the diagram opposite, process 1, Enter Orders, is to be exploded. The process is described below in detail.

Orders from customers comprise order details and, optionally, payment. Order details are checked for valid stock numbers. Orders failing this check are referred to the sales manager.

For cash sales, payments are checked against prices on the stock file. One of two 'payment advices' might be sent to the customer. Overpayments result in a credit being sent. Underpayments result in a payment request being sent, and the order is held awaiting correct payment. When the payment is correct, the order continues through the system.

For credit sales, credit status is checked by inspecting the payment history file. Rejected orders are referred to the sales manager.

Explode process 1, Enter Orders, to a lower-level diagram.

SOLUTION

Often the most difficult part of explosion is not drawing the child diagram, but linking it correctly to the parent diagram. Let's have a look at a solution to Exercise 4.1.

First, order details are checked for valid stock numbers, with rejected orders referred to the sales manager. This could be drawn as in Figure A.17. Notice that 'Stock Numbers' is a sub-flow of 'Stock Details' from the top-level diagram. Similarly, 'Order Details' is a sub-flow of 'Order'.

Next, payments are checked against prices on the stock file. The diagram could be extended as in Figure A.18. Again, the two inputs from the parent diagram are sub-flows.

When checking payments, over- or underpayments cause a payment advice to be sent to the customer. This extends the diagram as in Figure A.19.

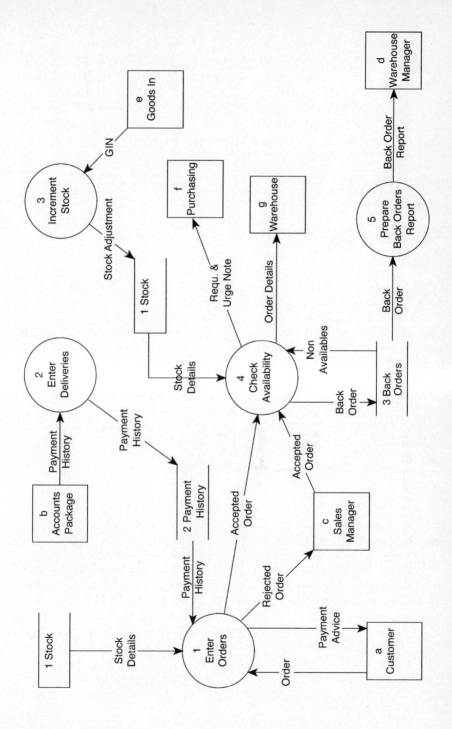

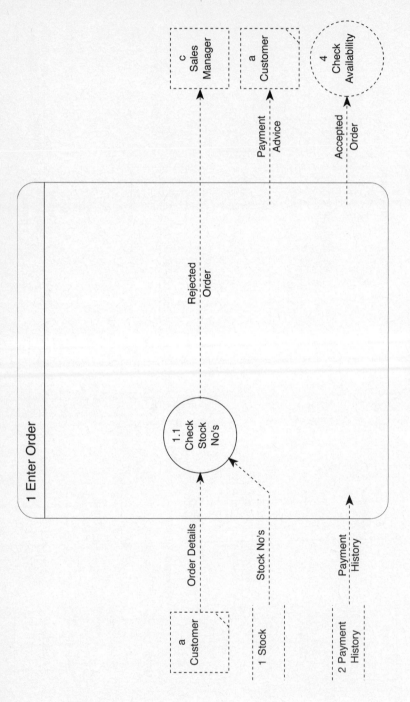

Figure A.17

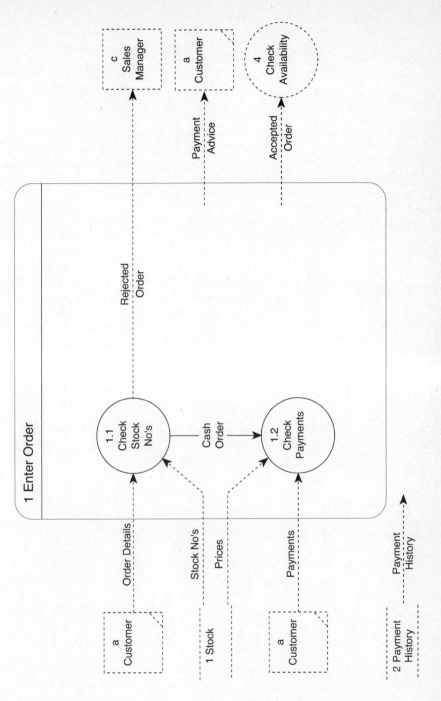

Figure A.18

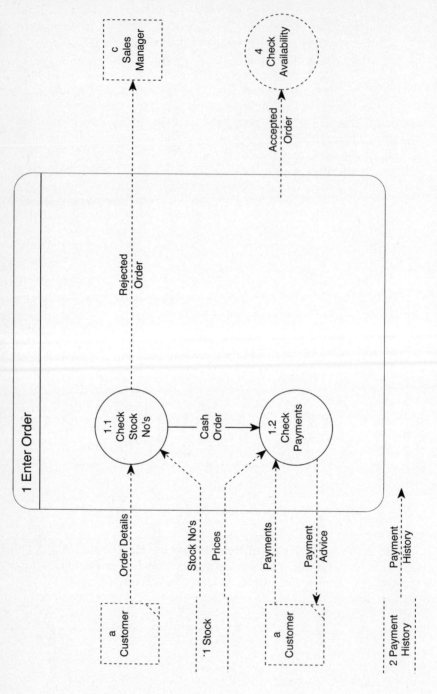

Figure A.19

For underpayments, orders are held awaiting correct payment. This could be drawn as in Figure A.20. Remember that it's not necessary to add the local data store 'Pending Orders' to the parent diagram.

When the payment's correct, the order continues through the system. We already have a process 'Check Payments' to do this, with 'Payment' as an input. All we need to add is a flow of 'Pending Orders' to check against these further payments. To complete the picture, 'Accepted Orders' are passed on to the next process at the top level (see Figure A.21).

For credit sales, credit status is checked by inspecting the Payment History store. This may be drawn as in Figure A.22. 'Rejected Orders' are referred back to the sales manager. Again, 'Accepted Orders' are passed on to the next process at the top level, and that completes the diagram.

Exercise 5.1

Develop a data structure for the report sample below and define the contained data structures and data elements.

Delivery times

BR.no.	Mon	Tue	Wed
1	0720 Fresh	0720 Fresh	0715 Fresh
	1307 Groc SO	1835 Bulk Ev	1235 Prom
2	0720 Fresh	0700 Fresh	0705 Fresh
	0750 Groc SO	1315 Groc	1420 Bulk
3	0720 Fresh	0710 Fresh	0715 Fresh
	1100 Groc SO	0515 Groc NT	1345 Groc
	1400 Groc	0515 Bulk NT	1415 Bulk

Fresh = Fresh Food   SO = Standing Order
Groc = Grocery   NT = Night Time
Bulk = Bulk Delivery   Ev = Evening
Prom = Promotion

The sample above just gives detail from the top left-hand corner of a typical report. Assume that there are always 13 branches on the report. Also assume that each branch always gets at least one delivery Monday to Saturday, and never more than five, and that there are no deliveries on Sundays.

SOLUTION

The sample shows a report of delivery times which gives the deliveries for each branch for each day of the week. We can see that a

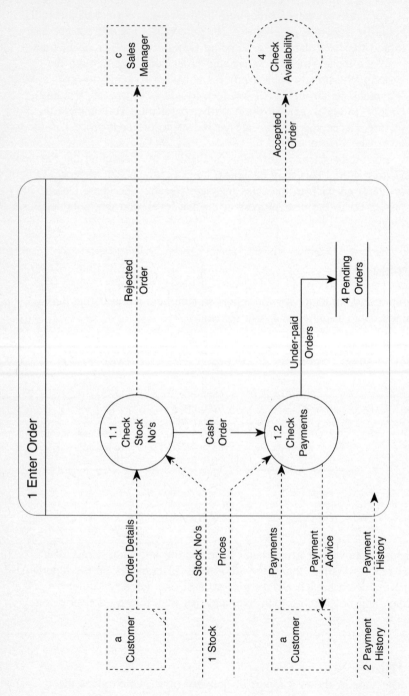

Figure A.20

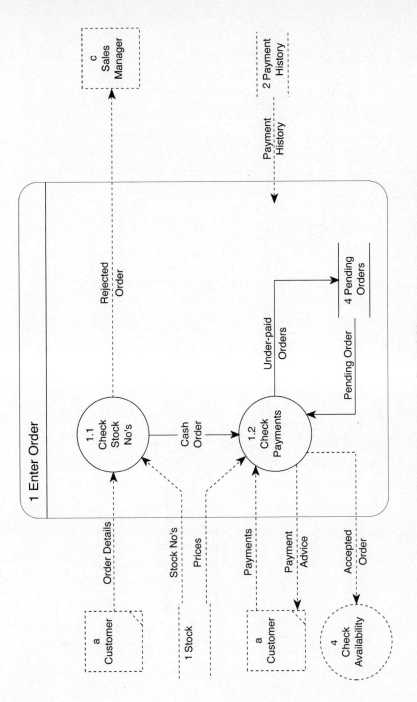

Figure A.21

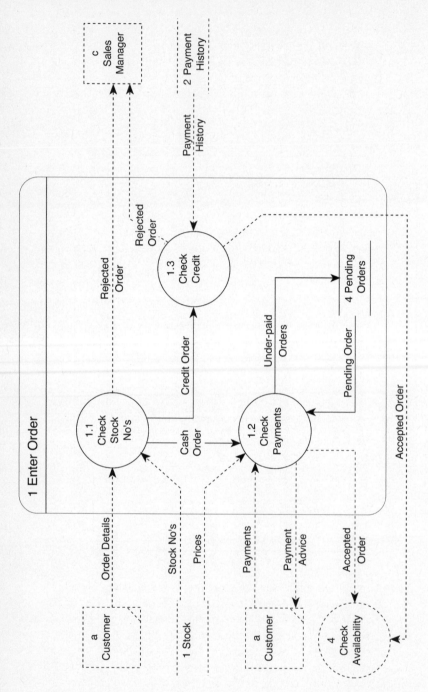

Figure A.22

branch may have more than one delivery in a day. For each delivery
we can see a time, a type of product, and, sometimes, a delivery code.

So, first we look at the structure of the report as a whole. At the
top level, we could consider the report to be an iteration of branch
delivery details. Therefore, we could start our data structure as
follows. The number of iterations is just the number of branches on
the report.

```
DELIVERY-TIMES
     BRANCH-DELIVERIES * (13)
```

Having dealt with the iteration of branch deliveries, we can
concentrate on the information for a single branch. That is, we're now
looking at the structure of a block across the report for a single
branch, for example:

2	0720 Fresh	0700 Fresh	0705 Fresh
	0750 Groc SO	1315 Groc	1420 Bulk

We could consider this to be a branch number, followed by an
iteration of daily delivery details (one for each day Monday to
Saturday). This would extend our data structure as follows:

```
DELIVERY-TIMES
     BRANCH-DELIVERIES * (13)
          BRANCH-NO
          DAILY-DELIVERIES * (6)
```

More simply, we might see the structure as a sequence: branch
number, followed by Monday's deliveries, followed by Tuesday's
deliveries, and so on. While this would not be incorrect, it would lead
to a somewhat unwieldy and repetitive data structure.

Having dealt with the iteration of daily deliveries, we can now
concentrate on the information for a single branch for a single day.
That is, we're now looking at the structure of a single cell on the
report, for example:

```
0700 Fresh
1315 Groc
```

The structure here is an iteration of individual deliveries. This would extend our data structure as follows. Notice that the iteration range this time is 1–5. This means that there is never less than one delivery per day for a branch and never more than five.

```
DELIVERY-TIMES
        BRANCH-DELIVERIES * (13)
            BRANCH-NO
            DAILY-DELIVERIES * (6)
                INDIVIDUAL-DELIVERIES * (1–5)
```

Again, more simply we might see this structure as a sequence: first delivery, followed by second delivery, and so on. But the iteration structure shown above would be preferable for the same reasons as before.

Having dealt with the iteration of individual deliveries, we can now concentrate on the information for a single branch, for a single day, for a single delivery. That is, we're now looking at the structure of a single delivery within a single cell. The structure here is just a sequence of Time, followed by Product Type, followed (optionally) by Delivery Code. This would extend our data structure as follows. Notice the square brackets round Delivery Code to show that it's not always present.

```
DELIVERY-TIMES
        BRANCH-DELIVERIES * (13)
            BRANCH-NO
            DAILY-DELIVERIES * (6)
                INDIVIDUAL-DELIVERIES * (1–5)
                    TIME
                    PRODUCT TYPE
                    [DELIVERY CODE]
```

We can now look at the completed structure and identify the data structures and data elements by remembering that data structures have sub-structures and data elements don't. We will assume that the top-level item, Delivery Times, is the flow or store on the DFD.

Therefore, Branch Deliveries, Daily Deliveries and Individual Deliveries are data structures. As their data dictionary entry is just a name, description and structure we won't go into these any further for this example.

The data elements in the structure are Branch Number, Time, Product Type and Delivery Code. The name, description and aliases are straightforward for these, so we'll just consider the values, length and cross-check information.

To find the values, and therefore the length, we need to consider whether each data element is discrete or continuous. We could consider the Branch Number to be continuous in the range 1–13. This would give us a length of two, because there are two digits in the maximum range limit.

Time is also continuous. We can see from the report sample that the 24-hour clock is being used, therefore the range would be 0000–2359. This gives us a length of four.

The Product Type is discrete. The 'codes' on the report are Fresh, Groc, Bulk and Prom. Their meanings are as given in the key at the bottom of the report. The longest code is 'Fresh' at five characters, so this gives us a length of five.

The Delivery Code is again discrete. The codes on the report are SO, NT and Ev. The meanings are again given in the key at the bottom. All three codes are two characters, so the length is two.

There are several cross-checks that we might investigate. For example, in the report we can see that all 'Fresh' deliveries are made before 09.00, and this might be checked. Also, time ranges might be defined for the Delivery Codes 'Evening' and 'Night-Time' to allow a cross-check between Time and Delivery Code.

Exercise 6.1

Produce Structured English for the process in the DFD below.

A sample of the Delivery Times report is shown below together with its data structure.

Delivery times

BR.no	Mon	Tue	Wed
1	1307 Groc SO	1835 Bulk Ev	1235 Prom
2	0750 Groc SO	1315 Groc	1420 Bulk
3	1100 Groc SO	0515 Groc NT	1345 Groc

(The sample just gives detail from the top left-hand corner of a typical report. Assume that there are always 13 branches on the report. Also assume that each branch always gets one delivery Monday to Saturday, and that there are no deliveries on Sundays.)

```
DELIVERY-TIMES
        BRANCH-DELIVERIES * (13)
                BRANCH-NO
                DAILY-DELIVERIES * (6)
                        TIME
                        PRODUCT
                        [DELIVERY CODE]
```

(The Delivery Times data structure shown above is a simplified version of the one developed as a solution to Exercise 5.1.)

The data structure for the flow into the process is shown below. The Standing Order flag in this data structure is set to 's' if the delivery is a Standing Order. Evening deliveries take place between 18.00 and 23.59. Night-time deliveries take place between 00.00 and 06.00.

```
DELIVERIES * (13)
        BRANCH-NO
        DAILY-DELIVERIES * (6)
                TIME
                PRODUCT
                STANDING ORDER
```

SOLUTION

The data structure for the report is basically an iteration of Branch Deliveries; each one comprising a Branch Number and an iteration of Daily Deliveries. Each Daily Delivery is made up of a sequence of Time, Product and, optionally, a Delivery Code.

The data structure of the Deliveries flow into the process from the Deliveries store is similar to the output flow. In both cases we have an iteration at the top level, comprising a Branch Number and an iteration of daily deliveries, first for Monday, then for Tuesday, and so on. . . Each Daily Delivery is then made up of Time and Product, as in the output data structure, but the last data element is different. Here we have a Standing Order flag, set to 'S' if the delivery is a standing order. This means that the other Delivery Codes on the report, Evening and Night-time, must be derived using the time.

So, now that we've thought carefully about the data, how do we build up the Structured English? Well, the report is basically some headings followed by an iteration of branch deliveries, so we might start as follows:

```
Write Headings
DOWHILE more Deliveries
        DO Output-Branch-Deliveries
ENDDO
```

The stop condition for the loop is 'when we get to the end of the input'; that is, when we get to the end of the Deliveries iteration. Therefore, our condition for the DOWHILE is as shown.

That completes the top level and we now have to think about 'Output-Branch-Deliveries'. For each branch we write the branch number followed by all the daily deliveries. The branch number is straightforward. To write all the daily deliveries, we need to read the iteration in the input flow and write a daily delivery for each occurrence. This could be specified as follows:

```
Output-Branch-Deliveries
        Write Branch-No
                DOWHILE more Daily-Deliveries
                        DO Output-Individual-Delivieries
                ENDDO
```

The only thing remaining now is how to write individual deliveries. Well, the time and product are trivial, they're just copied across from the input. We do need to specify how to get the Delivery Code though. If the Standing Order is 'S', the Delivery Code is 'SO'. If the Time is 18.00 to 23.59, the Delivery Code is 'EV'. And, if the time is 00.00 to 06.00, the Delivery code is 'NT'. So, 'Output-Individual-Deliveries' is as follows:

```
Output-Individual-Deliveries
        Print Time and Product
        IF Standing-Order = S
             Delivery Code = SO
        ENDIF
        IF Time = 1800–2359
             Delivery Code = EV
        ENDIF
        IF Time = 0000–0060
             Delivery-Code = NT
        ENDIF
```

Exercise 6.2

Develop a decision table and a decision tree for the problem statement below.

If the age of the main driver is 25 years or more, the car is manufactured in the UK and the accident record is good, the premium charged is 6% of the declared value and the policy issued is a comprehensive one. If the accident record is not good, the policyholder pays the first £50 of any damage sustained, the premium is raised to 7% and a comprehensive policy is issued.

If the age of the main driver is 25 years or more, the car is not manufactured in the UK and the accident record is good, the policyholder pays the first £50 of any damage sustained, the premium charged is 6% of the declared value and a comprehensive policy is issued. On the other hand, if all the above conditions apply except that the accident record is not good, the premium is raised to 7% and a third-party policy only is issued.

If the age of the main driver is less than 25 years, the car is manufactured in the UK and the accident record is good, the premium charged is 6% of the declared value and the policy issued is a comprehensive one. If the accident record is not good and all other conditions apply, the premium is raised to 7% and a third-party policy only is issued.

If the age of the main driver is less than 25 years, the car is not manufactured in the UK and the accident record is good, the policyholder pays the first £50 of any damage sustained, the premium charged is 8% of the declared value and a comprehensive policy is issued. If the accident record is not good and all other conditions apply, the clerk is instructed to decline the risk altogether and inform the applicant accordingly.

SOLUTION

The first thing to do is to extract the conditions. In the first sentence we find three conditions: the age and accident record of the driver, and the country of manufacture of the car. The rest of the problem statement only restates or negates these conditions in various combinations, so this results in a condition stub as follows:

> Age > = 25
> UK car
> 'good' accident record

There are three conditions, giving us eight rules. The condition entry can then be completed mechanically as in Table A.1.

For this example, there are seven separate actions that may be entered into the action stub as in Table A.2.

Most of these actions will be combined with others to satisfy the rules and there might have been a temptation to combine actions as in Table A.3. However, it's better to keep them separate, similarly to conditions, for simplicity and to give flexibility in the event of rule changes.

So, once the action stub has been sorted out, the action entry can be completed by matching the problem to the rules in the table. This gives us

Table A.1

	1	2	3	4	5	6	7	8
Age > = 25	Y	Y	Y	Y	N	N	N	N
UK car	Y	Y	N	N	Y	Y	N	N
'Good' accident record	Y	N	Y	N	Y	N	Y	N

Table A.2

	1	2	3	4	5	6	7	8
Age > = 25	Y	Y	Y	Y	N	N	N	N
UK car	Y	Y	N	N	Y	Y	N	N
'Good' accident record	Y	N	Y	N	Y	N	Y	N
6%								
7%								
8%								
Comprehensive								
Third party								
First £50								
Declined								

Table A.3

	1	2	3	4	5	6	7	8
Age > = 25	Y	Y	Y	Y	N	N	N	N
UK car	Y	Y	N	N	Y	Y	N	N
'Good' accident record	Y	N	Y	N	Y	N	Y	N
6% & comprehensive								
6% & comprehensive & £50								
7% % comprehensive								
7% & comprehensive & £50								
8% & comprehensive & £50								
7% & third party								
Declined								

a completed limited entry table as in Table A.4. Notice how the rules with more than one action are simply shown in the action entry by entering more than one cross.

There are one pair of rules in the table that can be consolidated. Rules 1 and 5 have the same actions and differ by only one condition. Therefore, they may be combined as in Table A.5.

Table A.4

	1	2	3	4	5	6	7	8
Age > = 25	Y	Y	Y	Y	N	N	N	N
UK car	Y	Y	N	N	Y	Y	N	N
'Good' accident record	Y	N	Y	N	Y	N	Y	N
6%	X		X		X			
7%		X		X		X		
8%							X	
Comprehensive	X	X	X		X		X	
Third party				X		X		
First £50		X	X				X	
Declined								X

Table A.5

	1/5	2	3	4	6	7	8
Age > = 25	–	Y	Y	Y	N	N	N
UK car	Y	Y	N	N	Y	N	N
'Good' accident record	Y	N	Y	N	N	Y	N
6%	X		X				
7%		X		X	X		
8%						X	
Comprehensive	X	X	X			X	
Third party				X	X		
First £50		X	X			X	
Declined							X

Table A.6

	1/5	2	3	4	6	7	8
Age > = 25	–	Y	Y	Y	N	N	N
UK car	Y	Y	N	N	Y	N	N
'Good' accident record	Y	N	Y	N	N	Y	N
Premium charged	6	7	6	7	7	8	–
Type of cover	C	C	C	3	3	C	–
First £50		X	X			X	
Declined							X

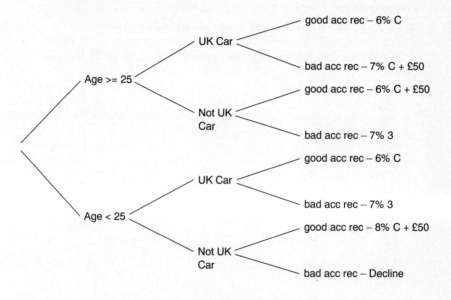

Figure A.23

Rules 4 and 6 have the same actions, but differ by two conditions, so they can't be consolidated. If we were to combine them, we would be saying that we were 'indifferent' to the two rules that didn't match. That is, any rules with an N against 'good accident record' should result in the actions (7%, third party). We can see by inspection of the table that this is not the case.

We might extend some of the entries as in Table A.6. We could then go on to express this as a decision tree as in Figure A.23.

Exercise 7.1

Draw an ERD for the following problem statement.

When the stock for an item is low, an order is made to the appropriate supplier and a copy of the Purchase Order is filed. When there are deliveries from suppliers, the items are checked against the relevant Purchase Orders, and added to stock.

SOLUTION

Let's go through this one sentence at a time and try to build up an ERD. The first sentence tells us 'When the stock for an item is low, an order is made to the appropriate supplier, and a copy of the Purchase Order is filed'. This gives us two entities, Item and Supplier, and a relationship, 'is ordered from', as in Figure A.24.

We can extend this with an associative object type, as in Figure A.25, because the relationship has its own data, a store of Purchase Orders.

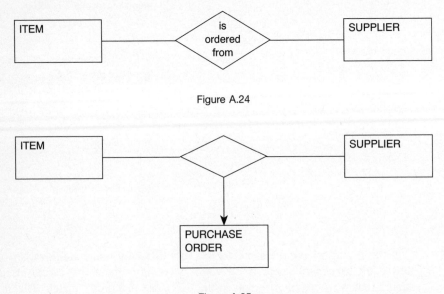

Figure A.24

Figure A.25

The next sentence says 'When there are deliveries from suppliers, the items are checked against the relevant Purchase Orders, and added to stock'. We have another potential entity here, Delivery, and we could add it to our diagram as in Figure A.26. This reads 'Supplier makes Delivery, Delivery is checked against Purchase Order, and Delivery is added to Item'. Note that Stock isn't another entity here, it's just an alias for the Item entity.

This works, but if we remember that it is the relationships that should record the events or transactions in the system, perhaps

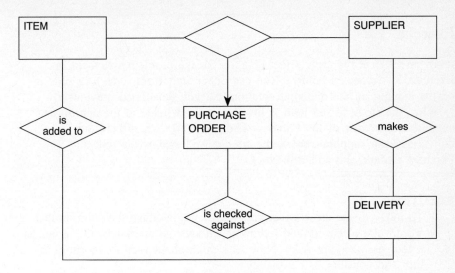

Figure A.26

deliveries are more like relationships. We can solve this by modelling
it as an associative object type, as in Figure A.27. Here Supplier
delivers Item, and the record of that transaction is a Delivery. We no
longer need the explicit relationship 'Delivery is added to Item' as this
is implied by 'Supplier delivers Item'. However, we do still need
'Delivery is checked against Purchase Order'.

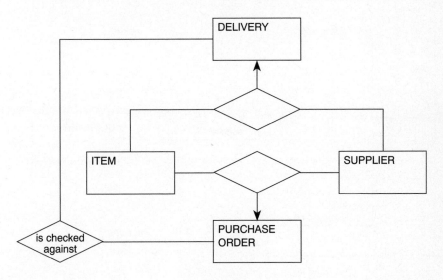

Figure A.27

Exercise 7.2

Draw an ERD in the crow's feet notation for the problem statement in Exercise 7.1 (repeated below). You can either start from scratch or base it on the diagram in the diamond notation that you developed previously.

When the stock for an item is low, an order is made to the appropriate supplier and a copy of the Purchase Order is filed. When there are deliveries from suppliers, the items are checked against the relevant Purchase Orders, and added to stock.

SOLUTION

To move to the crow's feet notation, if we just take the solution that we developed earlier and redraw it without the diamonds, this gives us a start as in Figure A.28. Now let's think about each relationship in turn and consider its cardinality.

First, the Item and Purchase Order entities. The relationship here is many to many because each item appears on many Purchase Orders and each Purchase Order has many items. The relationship between Purchase Order and Supplier is one to many because each Purchase Order is sent to one supplier and each supplier receives many Purchase Orders. The relationship is also one to many between Supplier and Delivery. Each Supplier makes many deliveries and each

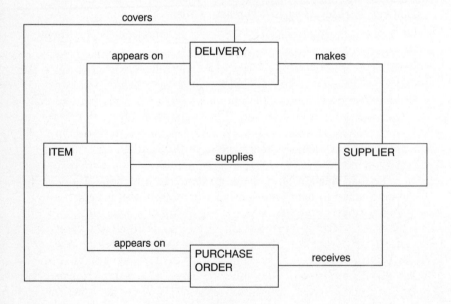

Figure A.28

delivery is made by one Supplier. The relationship between Item and Delivery is many to many. Each item appears on many deliveries and each delivery is made up of many items. This gives us a partly converted ERD as in Figure A.29.

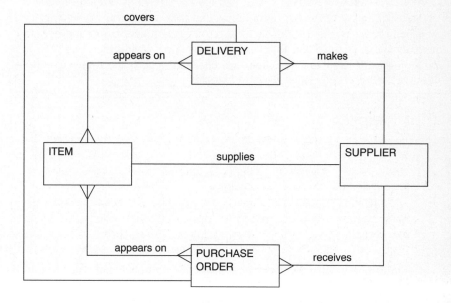

Figure A.29

The cardinality of the relationship between Delivery and Purchase Order would bear further investigation. If we could guarantee that each Purchase Order generated exactly one delivery, the relationship is one to one. However, it seems unlikely that all the items on a Purchase Order will always be sent in one delivery. Also, items from several Purchase Orders might be sent in the same delivery. If this is the case, we're looking at a many to many relationship. So, each delivery covers many Purchase Orders and each Purchase Order results in many deliveries.

The final relationship is between Item and Supplier. This is likely to be a many to many relationship where each item is supplied by many suppliers and each supplier supplies many items. It is unlikely that there would be only one supplier for an item or that suppliers supply only one item. This results in an ERD as in Figure A.30.

There are no one to one relationships here, so we just need to consider the removal of the many to many relationships to complete the diagram. Two of the entities involved, Delivery and Purchase Order, have repeating groups. In both cases there might be some static

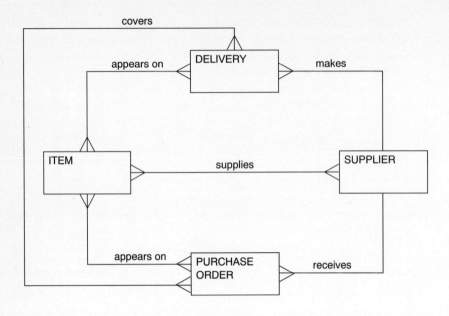

Figure A.30

information, like Delivery/Purchase Order number and date, followed by a repetition of information like item number and quantity for each item. Two of the many to many relationships could be removed quite simply by identifying entities for repeating groups. This would give us an ERD as in Figure A.31.

Reading these new relationships, each item appears on many delivery lines and each delivery line refers to one item. Each delivery has many delivery lines and each delivery line refers to one delivery. Each purchase order has many purchase order lines and each Purchase Order line relates to one Purchase Order. Each item appears on many purchase order lines and each purchase order line refers to one item.

The other two many to many relationships are not as straightforward to resolve. Neither the Item nor the Supplier entities have repeating groups, so the only option for resolution is a link entity type. The other relationship, between Purchase Order and Delivery looks more promising. Both entities have repeating groups that have already been removed as separate entities, and either might be able to resolve the relationship. If we look to use Delivery Line, we already have the one to many relationship from Delivery to Delivery Line in place, so we only need to add a one to many relationship from Purchase Order to Delivery Line as in Figure A.32.

Reading this relationship, each purchase order results in many delivery lines and each delivery line relates to one purchase order.

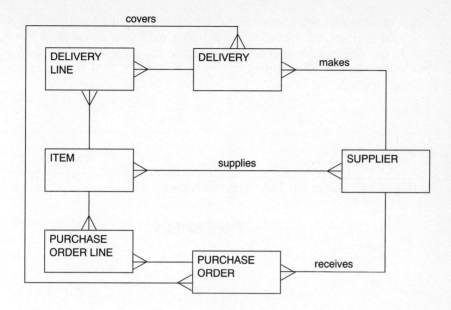

Figure A.31

Unfortunately, this might not be true. If orders for an item are accumulated from a number of purchase orders and delivered in one delivery, the delivery line would relate not to one Purchase Order, but to many. If this is the case, the many to many relationship between Delivery and Purchase Order can't be resolved using Delivery Line.

If we look to use Purchase Order Line, we would only have to add a one to many relationship from Delivery to Purchase Order Line, as in Figure A.33.

Reading this relationship, each delivery refers to many purchase order lines and each purchase order line results in one delivery.

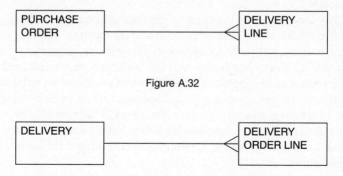

Figure A.32

Figure A.33

Unfortunately, this also might not be true. If an order for an item was split over several deliveries, the purchase order line would result not in one delivery but in many. To complete the diagram would clearly require further investigation, but we will leave the final version here as in Figure A.31.

Exercise 7.3

Normalize the data in the Time Sheet in Figure A.34.

TIME SHEET

Staff No :   Week No   :
Name   :   Grade   :
                                                   Hourly Rate :

Proj. Code	Project Title	Hrs Worked

Non Project Hrs

Total Hrs

Holidays :   Sick Leave :

Figure A.34

SOLUTION

Let's look at how to normalize the data on that Time Sheet. At the top we have a staff number and name on the left, and a week number, grade and hourly rate on the right. We get this information once for each time sheet. We'll assume that the hourly rate is entirely dependent on the grade. Under this there's a space to write the different projects that the person has worked on during the week. This is a repeating group of project code, project title and hours worked. At the bottom there are non-project hours, total hours, and holidays and sick leave for the week. Again, this information only occurs once per time sheet.

This gives us some unnormalized data, with one repeating group identified within the main relation:

```
Timesheet (Staff No, Name, Week No, Grade,
          Rate, (Proj-code, Proj-title, Proj-hrs),
          non-proj hrs, total hrs, holidays, sick
          leave)
```

The first step is to identify keys and remove repeating groups. The main key will be staff number and week number, because the time sheet is unique for a particular member of staff in a particular week. For the repeating group, project code will be the key:

```
Timesheet (Staff No, Name, Week No, Grade,
          Rate, (Proj-code, Proj-title, Proj-hrs),
          non-proj hrs, total hrs, holidays, sick
          leave)
```

When we remove the repeating group, this gives us two relations. The data is now in first normal form:

```
Timesheet (Staff No, Week No, Name, Grade, Rate, non-
          proj hrs, total hrs, holidays, sick leave)
Staff Project (Staff No, Week No, Proj-code, Proj-title,
          Proj-hrs)
```

The next step is to remove partial key dependencies. If we look at the first relation, the last four attributes are all dependent on the whole key. However, the first three attributes are only dependent on staff number. So, we can make another relation:

```
Timesheet (Staff No, Week No, non-proj hrs, total hrs,
          holidays, sick leave)
Staff Project (Staff No, Week No, Proj-code, Proj-title,
          Proj-hrs)
Staff (Staff No, Name, Grade, Rate)
```

If we look at the second relation, project hours is dependent on the whole key. That is, project hours relates to a particular person, in a particular week, on a particular project. However, project title is dependent only on project code, so it can be removed. The data is now in second normal form:

> Timesheet (<u>Staff No</u>, <u>Week No</u>, non-proj hrs, total hrs,
>   holidays, sick leave)
> Staff Project (<u>Staff No</u>, <u>Week No</u>, <u>Proj-code</u>, Proj-hrs)
> Staff (<u>Staff No</u>, Name, Grade, Rate)
> Project (<u>Proj-code</u>, Proj-title)

The last thing to do is to remove non-key dependencies. Two of the relations can't have any, because there is only one non-key attribute in both cases. In the first relation there are no non-key dependencies. In the other relation, rate is dependent on grade. So, we can remove it and the data is in third normal form:

> Timesheet (<u>Staff No</u>, <u>Week No</u>, non-proj hrs, total hrs,
>   holidays, sick leave)
> Staff Project (<u>Staff No</u>, <u>Week No</u>, <u>Proj-code</u>, Proj-hrs)
> Staff (<u>Staff No</u>, Name, Grade)
> Project (<u>Proj-code</u>, Proj-title)
> Grade rate (<u>Grade</u>, Rate)

Exercise 8.1

Orders are received from customers and validated against the Stock file to see if all the items exist. If they do not, the item is added to the Stock file. Each order is then checked for availability. Orders that can be supplied immediately have the order details sent to the warehouse and the Stock file is decremented accordingly. Orders that cannot be satisfied immediately are placed in a back orders file and a requisition note is sent to the Purchasing Department for the missing items. If the items are no longer supplied, the Purchasing Department sends back a Not Supplied note and the items are deleted from the Stock file. When items are received from suppliers, the Goods Inward Department completes a Goods Inward Note and the Stock file is incremented. Once a year there is a stock audit which results in an audit report to the warehouse manager. Any items not ordered in the last year are deleted from the Stock file. Any items where there is a discrepancy between the physical stock and the Stock file have their stock level adjusted on the Stock file.

A DFD of this scenario is given in Figure A.35.

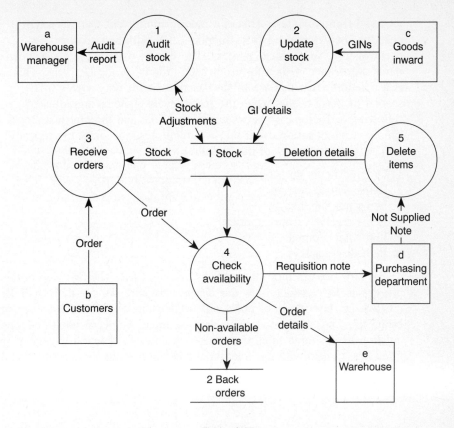

Figure A.35

Draw an entity life history for the Stock entity (assuming that there is an entity Stock on the ERD that matches the Stock store on the DFD).

SOLUTION

The first step is to draw up an event list from the problem statement and from looking at the effects on the Stock store on the DFD. The first event occurs at the 'Receive orders' process. New items are added to the Stock file if they do not exist. This is a creation event that we might describe 'ordered items not stocked'. The second event occurs at the 'Check availability' process. Here the Stock file is decremented for orders that can be satisfied immediately. This is a modification event that we might describe 'items sent to customer'. The third event occurs at the 'Delete items' process. Here, items are deleted from the Stock file if they are no longer supplied. This is a deletion event that we might describe 'items not supplied'. The fourth event occurs at the 'Update stock' process. Here the Stock file is updated when items are received from suppliers. This is a modification event that we might describe 'items received from supplier'. The fifth and sixth events occur at the 'Audit stock' process. The first of these takes place when items are deleted if they have not been ordered in the last year. This is a deletion event that we might describe 'items not ordered'. The second of these occurs when the stock levels of items are adjusted following a discrepancy between the stock file and the physical stock. This is a modification event that we might describe 'item discrepancy'.

This gives us an event list as follows:

1. Ordered items not stocked.
2. Items sent to customer.
3. Items not supplied.
4. Items received from supplier.
5. Items not ordered.
6. Item discrepancy.

We now need to turn this event list into an ELH. The first step in this process is to consider how the classic structure for an ELH will be created, i.e. how the root node will be decomposed into a sequence of birth, life and death nodes. In this example we have identified one creation event, three modification events and two deletion events. It is often best to deal with the creation and deletion events first, as they tend to be simpler, and come back to the modification events.

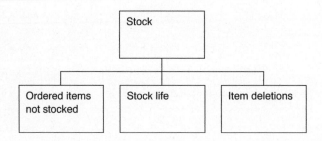

Figure A.36

So, the initial decomposition of the root node could be as in Figure A.36. That is, the life history of the stock entity is a sequence: 'Ordered items not stocked', followed by 'Stock life', followed by 'Item deletions'. There is only one creation event, so we have no more to do there, but there are two deletion events. This may be taken care of by a simple selection, as in Figure A.37.

We now need to consider the modification events: items sent to customers, items received from suppliers and item discrepancies. Basically these are different types of item adjustments, indicating that a

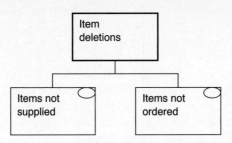

Figure A.37

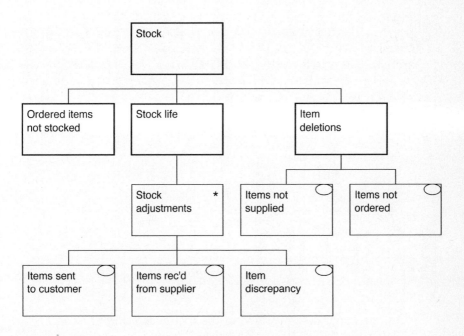

Figure A.38

selection is involved. There may be any number of adjustments, and they may occur in any order, indicating that an iteration is involved, but not a sequence. This is a common structure in ELHs and may be drawn as in the final ELH in Figure A.38. This is a classic ELH structure, with

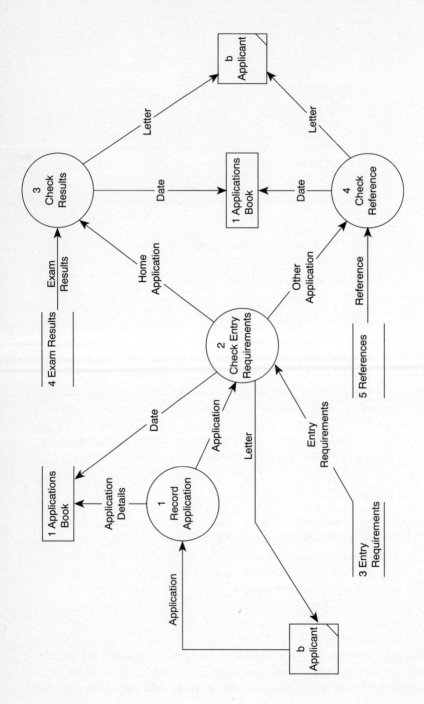

Figure A.39

creation and deletion events to the left and right respectively, and the main life of the entity modelled as an iteration of different types of transaction.

Exercise 9.1

Draw a structure chart from the DFD in Figure A.39.

SOLUTION

The first thing that we want to do in moving towards a structure chart is to redraw the DFD without the stores and externals. This gives us a stripped DFD as in Figure A.40.

Now we want to identify the central transform. The only process that we could say is definitely outside is Record Application. This is just logging the input before the main processing starts. The other three processes are all carrying out what we might consider to be the main work of the system. This is borne out graphically, because this is a busy group of processes.

The next step is to pick a boss module. Within the central transform, the best candidate is Check Entry Requirements. This is the busiest process and handles all applications, whereas the other two handle only some, which effectively rules them out. This would give us a start to our structure chart as in Figure A.41. The alternative is to create a new boss module. This would give us a structure chart as in Figure A.42.

There's not really much to choose between these, but we'll continue with the second option so that we can follow through the development of a structure chart with a new boss module as an alternative to the example in the chapter. Notice how the modules from the central transform communicate via the boss module rather than directly.

We now add some structure chart details, redrawing the processes as modules, and replacing the flows with connections and data couples, as in Figure A.43. The module 'Check Reference' looks a little out of place here, as if it is a human process from a current logical DFD that will not be automated. However, if we consider that its concerns are not the human activity of actually checking the references and making a decision, but the administrative processes associated with this (e.g. producing letters, updating dates) then there is no problem.

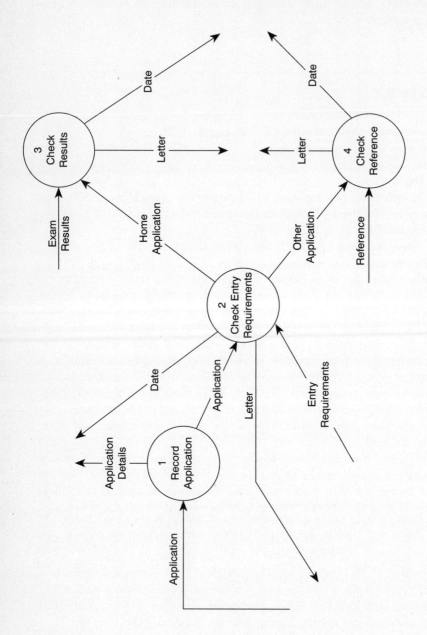

Figure A.40

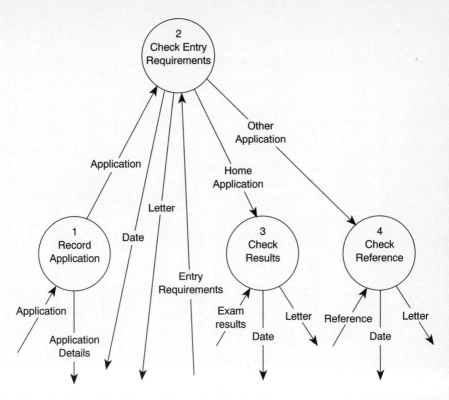

Figure A.41

There is only one control couple that we might want to add, to say
that we've got to the end of the stream of applications if they are
being processed as a batch. Also, we want to tidy up the loose ends
with read and write modules (see Figure A.44).

Notice that we've made a distinction between Write Applications
Book, which writes all the application details to the Applications
Book, and Update Applications Book, which merely updates that store
with a date. Perhaps this is not really necessary as both modules use
the same data store, but as we saw in Chapter 9, each module should
have a single, definable function.

This is acceptable for an initial solution, but it's rather messy and
there's a fair amount of duplication. There's a couple of things that
we might do to revise this first-cut structure chart. First, there doesn't
seem to be any good reason why Record Application should be
subordinate to Check Entry Requirements. This is just one of the

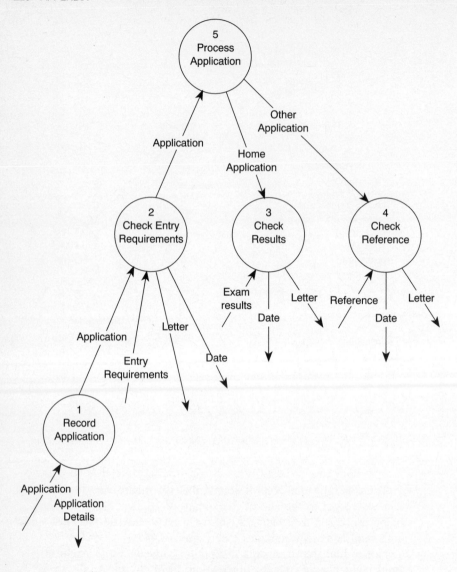

Figure A.42

processes carried out on applications in the system. So, we could call Record Application directly from the boss module as in Figure A.45.

Effectively, we've just pruned a branch from Check Entry Requirements and grafted it onto the boss module. This works well, but we must provide for a way for a way for applications to get to

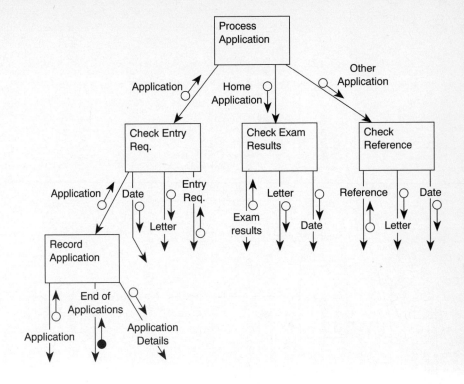

Figure A.43

'Check Entry Requirements' now that they are not passed directly
from 'Record Application' as in Figure A.44. This is achieved by
adding a data couple 'Applications' from the boss module to 'Check
Entry Requirements'. Applications now reach the boss module directly
as a result of the pruning and grafting.

The second item that we might want to revise is the duplication and
multiple calls to two of the modules. 'Write Letter' is shown three
times. We don't have to implement this as identical pieces of code
duplicated a number of times. We could have one piece of code with
a number of calls to it, as long as we're happy that the code always
executes in the same way on the same input parameters. We could
also draw the module just once and link into it a number of times, as
we have with 'Update Applications Book', but this can be messy and
make for crossing lines. For example, we couldn't have dealt tidily
with both 'Write Letter' and 'Update Applications Book' in this way
on this structure chart.

An alternative would be to take out these modules and control them
from the boss module. This would cause the structure chart to change

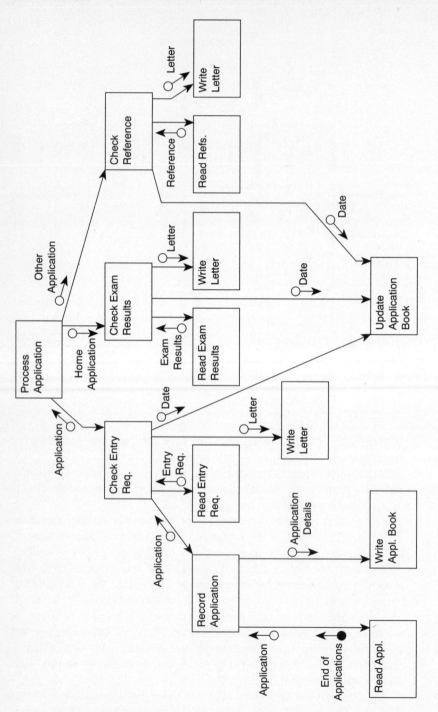

Figure A.44

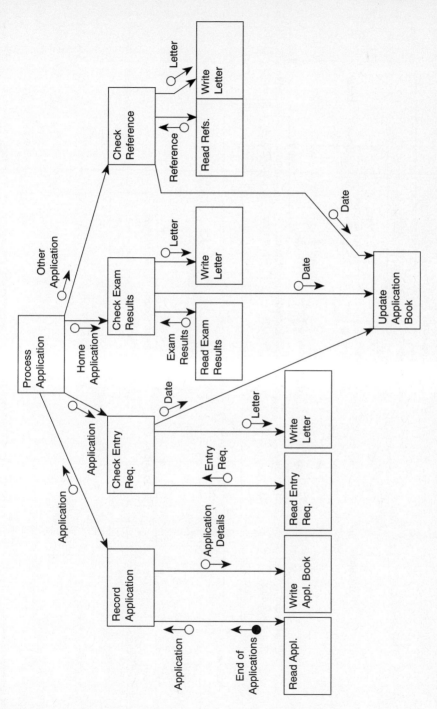

Figure A.45

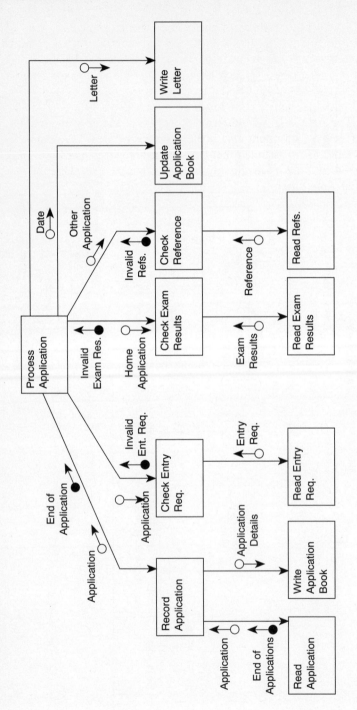

Figure A.46

as in Figure A.46. This tidies up the structure chart because the modules now appear only once and are called only once. Notice that we have to pass some more information up to the boss module to allow this to happen. On each leg where the modules used to appear previously, after the application has been passed down, a flag is passed back to report on the result of the check (i.e. the flags Invalid Entry Requirements, Invalid Exam Results and Invalid References). Perhaps some data might also need to be passed to allow completion of the letter? It is assumed that the Application itself does not need to be passed back as it has already been through the boss module and could be stored there.

Bibliography

Ashworth and Slater (1993), *An Introduction to SSADM Version 4*, McGraw-Hill

Boehm (1976) 'Software Engineering', *IEEE Transactions on Computers*, December

Dahl, Dijkstra and Hoare (1972) *Structured Programming*, Academic Press

De Marco (1978) *Structured Analysis and System Specification*, Yourdon Press

Gane and Sarson (1977) *Structured Systems Analysis*, IST

Griffiths and Lockyer (1992) Structured Methods and CASE Tools videos, University of Teesside

Jackson (1975) *Principles of Program Design*, Academic Press

Jackson (1983) *System Development*, Prentice Hall

Lockyer and Griffiths (1985–97) ASCENT CASE tool, University of Teesside

Olle *et al.*, (1988) *Information Systems Methodologies*, Addison-Wesley

Robinson and Prior (1995) *Systems Analysis Techniques*, Thomson

Ross (1977) 'Structured Analysis' *IEEE Transactions on Software Engineering*, January

Ward and Mellor (1986) *Structured Analysis of Real Time Systems*, Yourdon Press

Yourdon and Constantine (1975) *Structured Design*, Yourdon Press

Yourdon (1975) *Structured Walkthroughs*, Yourdon Press

Yourdon (1989) *Modern Structured Analysis*, Prentice Hall

Index